VEGETABLE
GARDENING
for
ONTARIO

Laura Peters

LONE
PINE

Lone Pine Publishing

Lone Pine Publishing
10145 – 81 Avenue
Edmonton, AB T6E 1W9
Canada
Website: www.lonepinepublishing.com

Library and Archives Canada Cataloguing in Publication

Peters, Laura, 1968-
        Vegetable gardening for Ontario / Laura Peters.

Includes index.
ISBN 978-1-55105-863-4

        1. Vegetable gardening--Ontario. I. Title.

SB323.C3P47 2011   635.09713   C2010-906918-8

Editorial Director: Nancy Foulds
Project Editor: Sheila Quinlan
Photo Coordinator and Editorial Support: Kelsey Everton
Production Manager: Gene Longson
Layout and Production: Janina Kuerschner
Production Support: Kamila Kwiatkowska
Cover Design: Gerry Dotto

Photos: All photos are by Laura Peters except: All America Selections 163b, 227b; Sandra Bit 6; Franky De Meyer 97a; Tamara Eder 17, 46, 50, 55a, 185b; Elliot Engley 31, 32; Jen Fafard 42, 104, 127; Derek Fell 24, 35, 64, 65a&b, 67b, 71b, 73, 100b, 118a, 119, 139a, 149b, 169a&b, 177, 185a, 187a, 205, 211, 212, 223a, 224b, 229a&b, 230, 231a&b, 232, 233, 234a&b, 235, 236, 237, 251, 253, 254, 255; Saxon Holt 163a, 164a&b, 203, 213, 252; iStock 1, 117a, 201b, 228, 258; Liz Klose 48, 89a, 141a, 189a, 220b, 239b; Trina Koscielnuk 120; Scott Leigh 113; Janet Loughrey 77a; Tim Matheson 25, 26, 27, 30a&b, 40, 44, 45a, 49, 52a, 55b, 56, 58; Marilyn McAra 168b; Kim O'Leary 53; photos.com 3, 60, 61, 115b, 199; Robert Ritchie 52b, 57; Nanette Samol 4, 21, 33, 34, 41, 62, 63, 68, 72, 76, 78a, 80, 84, 85b, 88, 89b, 90, 91b, 92, 94, 95, 96, 98, 100a, 102a&b, 103, 105b, 106a, 107b, 112, 114, 115a, 116, 117b, 118b, 122a, 124, 128, 130, 133, 136, 138, 140, 144, 146, 148, 149a, 150a, 151, 153a&b, 154a&b, 156, 159a, 160a, 162, 165, 166, 167a, 168a, 170b, 171, 172, 174, 178, 181b, 183a, 184, 186a&b, 187b, 188, 194, 200, 204, 206a, 207a, 208, 210, 214, 219, 223b, 225a, 226, 238, 240b, 241a, 242b, 245a, 246, 256; Paul Swanson 39a,b,c&d, 66, 67a, 74a&b, 78b, 99, 109, 123, 126b, 137, 139b, 141b, 142a, 145, 147a&b, 160b, 179, 189b, 190b, 192a, 193a, 198a&b, 206b, 207b, 239a, 250; Sandy Weatherall 11, 12, 18, 20, 29, 43, 79, 86, 97b, 101, 106b, 108a&b, 110, 111a, 132a, 135a, 152, 167b, 170a, 175, 176a, 218, 220a, 241b, 243a, 248, 249; Don Williamson 54.

Maps (pp. 8, 9): adapted from Natural Resources Canada

We acknowledge the financial support of the Government of Canada through the Canada Book Fund (CBF) for our publishing activities.

PC: 15

Contents

Introduction

Vegetable gardens have been part of human culture for thousands of years. Along with harnessing fire, developing the wheel and domesticating animals, cultivating food is one of the benchmarks of human advancement. Growing plants that provide food and learning to store it for times of scarcity allowed humans to develop civilizations.

When we buy food from the grocery store, we give little thought to where it came from, how far it had to travel and how much it cost to transport it, first to the store and then to the table. We don't think about how it was grown or who grew it. When we grow our own food plants, we develop a greater appreciation for the food, our gardens and our own ability to provide for ourselves and our families.

There are many good reasons to grow your own vegetables: you can save money on your grocery bill; it's environmentally friendly because fewer resources will be used in growing and getting the food to your table; it saves wildlife habitat by reducing the need to expand cultivated land; and it gives you a chance to seek out varieties and specialty items. An additional, often-overlooked reason to grow vegetables is that they are attractive and often unique in appearance.

Vegetable plants vary in size, colour and texture and often have wonderful flowers, stunning foliage or decorative fruit in colours and shapes not often replicated in ornamental plants.

Many gardeners are put off by the thought of digging up a square or rectangle and having an uninspiring display of rows in their carefully landscaped garden. Vegetable gardening doesn't have to be this way. When you look at a vegetable plant, don't think just about the end result; also think about the appearance of the plant and what it can add to

your ornamental garden. Plenty of edible plants can be added to the landscape you already have. They don't have to be planted in rows; single plants and small groups can make attractive features (see Choosing Your Style, page 10, for more information). Also, pests and diseases are less likely to affect your entire crop if certain plant types are spread out in groups here and there rather than all together in one location.

Ontario is an ideal place to grow a huge variety of vegetables, so think about your favourites. You

Vegetables, like this lettuce, don't have to be grown in rows.

don't have to try to accommodate your food needs for an entire year, but you could supplement what you buy by growing a few plants. Do you eat a lot of broccoli? Three to six plants can provide two people with a lot of meals because many selections produce additional smaller heads once the main one is cut. A container of tomatoes combined with flowering annuals on a sunny balcony or deck is beautiful and functional. Four zucchini plants will leave you wondering what to do with all your extra zucchini.

Overall, Ontario is a fantastic province in which to garden, though the cold winter weather and relatively short growing season in many regions do present some challenges. Luckily, many vegetables like to grow in a climate where summer temperatures are moderate and the days are long. Some vegetables grow equally well in all parts of Ontario, despite the wealth of diverse growing conditions found here—almost every gardening situation imaginable within a country, much less a province.

The diversity in Ontario is wide and spans an expansive area. There are the fertile and deep floodplains that border the St. Lawrence River. Gardeners on the Canadian Shield generally have acidic and fertile but rocky soils, whereas those living around Georgian Bay and the Great Lakes may have sandy or rocky soils. Southern Ontario has mostly alkaline, less rocky soil and milder winters, thanks to the moderating effect

Zucchini plants can be very prolific.

of the Great Lakes. Each region of the province provides a niche in which a select few vegetables excel.

Despite the regional characteristics and limitations imposed by broad factors such as climate, season length and day length, conditions can deviate greatly from garden to garden within a region. The details of soil conditions, garden micro-climates, light and heat influence your garden regardless of where you are in the province. These factors can vary not only from garden to garden but also within a single garden.

The three most important pieces of climate information are the hardiness zone, the last frost date of spring and the first frost date of fall for your region. These are not hard and fast numbers but are excellent guidelines that will help you choose plants and plan your garden. Hardiness zones are based on winter temperatures (see map, below) and are relevant mostly for perennial vegetables. Plants are rated based on the hardiness zones in which they will grow. The frost dates are a good estimate of season length (see map, right). If you can only depend on four frost-free months, you may want to choose plants that will survive a light frost or that will mature during your anticipated growing season.

The frost dates also ultimately affect when you will begin to seed, whether it's indoors or out. Often you will be instructed to start seeds

Plant hardiness zones for Ontario

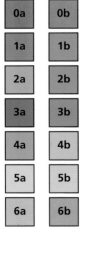

Average annual frost-free days for Ontario

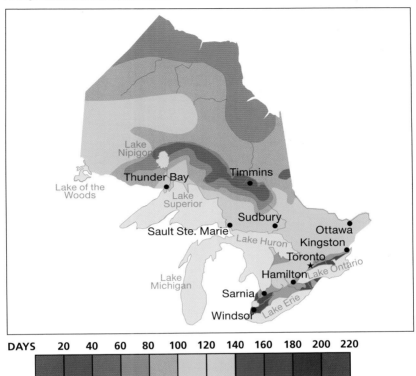

a number of weeks before the last frost date, and this date is crucial to the end result: the harvest. If you don't allow enough time for the plant to produce, then you will end up with a great-looking, leafy vegetable garden, but little in the way of produce to harvest, particularly when it comes to longer season veggies. Too short a season is a dealbreaker in the world of vegetable gardening.

Depending on the vegetable in question, hardiness zones and frost dates provide a good starting point but should not completely rule your planting decisions. An early, warm spring is an excellent opportunity to get a jump on the growing season, while a cold, wet, late spring might mean waiting a week or two more than you expected. If you plant certain seedlings out too early, and they're hit by frost, your efforts and your budget will have been for naught.

As with any gardening, growing vegetables should be fun. They can add unique colours and textures to your garden and your dinner plate. Experiment with a few each year, and you may soon find yourself looking for space to add even more.

A traditional row

Choosing Your Style

Vegetable gardens come in many forms and include a wide variety of plants. The neat rows of a traditional vegetable garden were adopted from the farm garden, and the attention paid to plant and row spacing is designed to make large numbers of plants more easily accessible. If you have plenty of space and want loads of vegetables to store over winter, this style can work for you and is still preferred by many gardeners.

There is no need to segregate vegetables from ornamental plants. The French potager, or kitchen garden, is a garden that is both decorative and functional. It generally consists of a symmetrical arrangement of raised beds. Plants are often repeated in a location in each bed rather than having one bed of all the same plant. Vegetables are combined with herbs and fruiting shrubs as well as edible flowers.

In intensive gardens, plantings are made in groups rather than rows. They may be formal or informal. An example of a more formal intensive garden is a square-foot garden. A square raised bed measuring 4 feet (1.2 metres) along each side is divided into 16 planting squares. Each square is planted with as much of a single crop as the space will allow. As soon as a crop has

Block planting

matured and been harvested, something new is planted to replace it as long as the growing season allows. An informal intensive garden could resemble a cottage-style garden, with vegetables planted in groups and drifts throughout the beds, but tucking groups of vegetables into existing beds could also be formal, depending on the nature of your garden.

As your garden grows and develops and you need to add new plants, think about adding edible ones. If you are replacing an existing perennial or shrub, perhaps you could replace it with asparagus, fiddlehead ferns or rhubarb—all sturdy, hardy perennial choices. The wealth of annual options is nearly limitless.

Raised Bed Gardening

Raised beds are an ideal way to grow vegetables. Gardening in raised beds means less work. Beds can be raised up to whatever height suits you. I built raised vegetable beds at my parents' place years ago because sore knees and bad backs meant they were physically unable to garden at ground level anymore. When you raise the level of the garden, there's little need to bend over or squat, and with the addition of a shallow ledge on all sides, a gentle bend is all it takes to weed or harvest a metre-high vegetable bed. In fact, the need for weeding will be drastically reduced. Overall, raised beds are incredibly tidy.

A raised bed

Also, the season can be extended somewhat by growing your vegetables in raised beds simply because they thaw out earlier than the ground itself. Granted it's not a huge difference, but sometimes every day counts in the growing season.

Growing vegetables in raised beds will have you asking yourself why you didn't build them sooner. As long as the drainage is adequate (leave the bottom open without sealing it or closing it in), the light exposure is good and the height suits you and what you're growing, go forth and see for yourself how wonderful they really are.

Vegetable Gardening with Limited Space

There are many options for gardeners with limited gardening space. With populations growing and city densities increasing, more and more

Tomatoes do very well in containers.

people are learning about the possibilities of their small spaces and discovering just how productive they can be. You don't need a large backyard to grow vegetables—you just need to get creative. Vegetables can grow in just about any space, whether in the ground or in some form of container. Food security is becoming more and more of an issue; growing even 1 to 5 percent of your produce will cut down on carbon emissions, your grocery bill and your time spent running to the store for something that could be right outside your door.

Intensive garden plots are becoming more and more popular, and for good reason. We don't always have a lot of space or time, but we want a fair to good return. Square-foot gardening is worth looking into, as it requires little space to produce a lot of vegetables, and other edible plants as well. Containers can be placed anywhere and take up little space, can

be moved around and sometimes offer more control than gardening directly in the ground. Just about anything can be used as a container, as long as there is adequate drainage and enough space for the vegetable plant that will be spending its life there. Use a good quality potting soil for containers, and add compost to the mix as a natural source of nutrients. Stay away from the potting soils with added synthetic fertilizers, moisture crystals and so on—keep it simple. Do not use soil from the garden, as it can compact, making it tough for roots to thrive.

Apartment and condominium dwellers should not shy away from growing vegetables. I currently have my vegetable garden on the balcony of my south-facing condo. Everything is grown in pots, and I have a steady stream of vegetables to pick, from early on in the season to last frost. I just have to be careful to leave

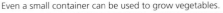
Even a small container can be used to grow vegetables.

Use containers to turn your balcony into a garden (above).

Vertical gardening expands your garden space upward.

myself enough room to walk through the maze of pots for watering, fertilizing and harvesting. Even if you decide to grow only one tomato plant on your patio, front porch or balcony, you will find yourself planning to grow more and more as the years go on.

Condominium owners will sometimes have a rooftop to garden on. Run the idea of growing vegetables on the rooftop by your condo board or strata council. People often jump on board immediately when they find out that they can grow food mere steps away from their front door, and they'll help to set it up and maintain the plants so that they can reap the rewards at harvest.

If the only open space you have is vertical, then vertical gardening is the solution. Smaller, trailing and leafy plants can all be grown in containers that hang or attach to a wall or other vertical surface, such as a fence. I've even known people to grow small plants or vegetables that produce on vines in old eaves troughs that were attached to the wall. They're ideal for successive sowings and they're out of the way, not to mention incredibly easy to get to and pick from. Trellises, pyramids, obelisks and other vertical supports are great for vegetables that can grow upward rather than outward, rendering your precious space more efficient and resulting in higher yields and easier harvesting. For example, beans, peas and cucumbers are great for supports such as netting, trellises and chainlink fences. Even hanging baskets are ideal for vertical spaces. Tomatoes are a common plant for such a container, whether they're a cascading cherry variety or an upright beefsteak type. Vertical gardening is of benefit to tomatoes because if left to flop on the ground, the air circulation is diminished, resulting in rot and insect infestation. Either way, as long as the right elements are present, anything is possible.

Community gardens are another option for those who just do not have the space but really want to grow some of their own food. Community gardens are everywhere, from the smallest towns to the largest cities, and have so much more to offer than just a plot. It's an inexpensive, fun way to garden and to meet others who share your desire to be more self-sufficient. Be sure that water is available close by so you're not hauling it from afar, and be brave and get involved with your community. If you have too much at harvest time,

donate it to your family, neighbours or the food bank. It doesn't take long to grow more than you can eat, and there is always someone who will appreciate the donation of delicious, nutritious, organic, locally grown produce…and you can claim responsibility for doing something really great.

Then there are Community Shared Agricultural (CSA) gardens. These are relatively new in Canada, and sometimes you have to search them out, but for anyone interested in growing vegetables in a space owned by someone else, a CSA garden is the perfect option because you still

Participating in a community garden can be fun and rewarding.

Community gardens are a great option for city dwellers with limited space.

Try growing your vegetables organically.

end up with yummy produce, and you get to participate in the process. CSA gardens are usually started by a local farmer or grower who decides to grow vegetables for a group that wants a specific amount of food on a weekly basis throughout the growing season. This agreement entails that you participate or volunteer some of your time to help out with the process, such as weeding, planting and harvesting. It's a great opportunity to support local, often organic agriculture, and you learn how the process works without having any soil or all of the work. You can find out more about locations throughout the province online at csafarms.ca/index.html.

Organic Gardening

The definition of "organic gardening" or "organic" varies globally, based on standards, regulations and

Produce is healthier when grown organically, without the use of synthetic chemicals.

laws. The basis of organic gardening is defined as a method of raising plants without the usage of synthetic pesticides or fertilizers; however, this definition has evolved into varied practices around the world. So what does our government constitute as organic? According to the Canadian Organic Growers, "Organic agriculture is a production system that sustains the health of soils, ecosystems and people. It relies on ecological processes, biodiversity and cycles adapted to local conditions, rather than the use of inputs with adverse effects. Organic agriculture combines tradition, innovation and science to benefit the shared environment and promote fair relationships and a good quality of life for all involved."

Organic gardening is a way to control weeds, diseases and pests by encouraging beneficial insect populations and supporting the relationship between host and predator, thereby using biological forms of control without harming the environment. Soil fertility should be maintained by maximizing biological soil activity. Plant and animal wastes should always be suitably selected and rotated from one location to another. Ecosystems should be created with sustainability in mind.

Gardening organically is of benefit to every living creature, but even more so when the end result is to be consumed. If you had been considering an organic garden in the past but felt too overwhelmed, there is no better place to begin than with growing vegetables. Being that the harvest will inevitably be eaten, isn't it worth it to grow the plants without the aid of synthetic chemicals of any kind? Isn't it always better to break everything down to its simplest form in the interests of good health? If for no other reason, try gardening organically for an experiment and see what you think; are the vegetables better tasting, adequate in size and so on? Even if you find little to no difference, your experiment will have resulted in ingesting fewer toxins, if any, and how can that be bad?

Organic gardening is healthy for you and for the environment.

Getting Started

Finding the right vegetables for your garden requires experimentation and creativity. Before you start planting, consider the growing conditions in your garden; these conditions will influence not only the types of plants you select, but also the location in which you plant them. Plants will be healthier and less susceptible to problems if grown in optimum conditions. It is difficult to significantly modify most of your garden's existing conditions; an easier approach is to match the plants to the garden.

Your plant selection will be influenced by the levels of light in your garden; the porosity, pH and texture of the soil; the amount of exposure in your garden; and the plants' tolerance to frost. Sketching your garden may help you visualize how various conditions might affect your planting decisions. Note shaded areas, low-lying or wet areas, exposed or windy areas, etc. Understanding your garden's growing conditions will help you learn where plants will perform best and prevent you from making costly mistakes.

Before you plant cabbage, make sure you have the ideal spot in your garden for it.

Light

There are four basic levels of light in a garden: full sun, partial shade (partial sun), light shade and full shade. Buildings, trees, fences and the position of the sun at different times of the day and year affect available light. Knowing what light is available in your garden will help you determine where to place each plant.

Plants in full sun locations, such as along south-facing walls, receive more than six hours of direct sunlight during the day. Locations classified as partial shade, such as east- or west-facing walls, receive direct sunlight for part of the day (four to six hours) and shade for the rest. Light shade locations receive shade for most or all of the day, but some sunlight does filter through to ground level. An example of a light shade location would be the ground under a small-leaved tree such as a birch. Full shade locations, which include the north side of a house, receive no direct sunlight.

Most vegetables thrive in full sun.

Soil

Soil quality is an extremely important element of a healthy garden. Plant roots rely on the air, water and nutrients that are held within soil. Plants also depend on soil to hold them upright. The soil in turn benefits from plant roots breaking down large clumps while preventing erosion by binding together small particles and by reducing the amount of exposed surface. When plants die and break down, they add organic nutrients to soil and feed beneficial microorganisms.

Soil is made up of particles of different sizes. Sand particles are the largest—water drains quickly from sandy soil, and nutrients tend to get washed away. Sandy soil does not compact very easily because the large particles leave air pockets between them. Clay particles are the smallest and can be seen only through a microscope. Clay holds the most nutrients, but it also compacts easily and has few air spaces. Clay is slow to absorb water and equally slow to let it drain. Silt is midway between sand and clay in particle size. Most soils are a combination of these three particles and are called loams.

Healthy soils smell sweet and nutty, and they contain a wide variety of particle sizes, shapes and weights. More importantly, healthy soils are teeming with life—fat earthworms, tiny microarthropods, such as spiders and mites, and organisms seen only with a microscope, including one-celled protozoa, fungal mycelia and myriads of bacteria. In healthy soils, the cycle of life is constantly turning, recycling dead matter into fuel for live matter. Precious minerals are continuously returned to the topsoil, and nutrients are released by all of the organisms that reside in the soil.

However, most soils, particularly those in your own backyard, are completely void of any life, depleted of organic matter, and are merely a medium that holds struggling plants upright. Dead soils are often the result of neglect, lack of knowledge of what it takes to maintain

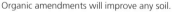

Organic amendments will improve any soil.

a living soil, erosion, devastated soil structure and synthetic chemical usage including fertilizers and pesticides. Plants grown in these soils are compromised and vulnerable. Insects and diseases are attracted to weak, struggling plants, and anything trying to survive in lifeless soil is bound to be attacked long before healthy plants in living soils are even considered as potential victims. Dead soils are an equation for disaster, but the addition of organic matter can turn these lifeless soils back into balanced, living communities of creatures large and small.

It is also important to consider the pH level (the scale on which acidity or alkalinity is measured) of soil, which influences the availability of nutrients. Most plants thrive in soil with a pH between 5.5 and 7.5. Soil pH varies a great deal from place to place in Ontario. Testing kits can be purchased at most garden centres, and soil-testing labs can analyze the pH and the quantities of various nutrients in your soil. The acidity of soil can be reduced with the addition of horticultural lime or wood ashes and increased with the addition of sulphur, peat moss or pine needles. For plants that prefer a pH that varies greatly from that of your garden soil, use planters or create raised beds so it is easier to control and alter the pH level of the soil.

Water drainage is affected by soil type and the terrain in your garden. Plants that prefer well-drained soil and do not require a large amount of moisture grow well on a sloping hillside garden with rocky soil. Water retention in these areas can be improved through the addition of organic matter. Plants that thrive on a consistent water supply or in boggy conditions are ideal for low-lying areas that retain water for longer periods or that hardly drain at all. In extremely wet areas, you can improve drainage by adding gravel, creating raised beds or using French drains or drainage tile.

Potatoes prefer an acidic soil.

Exposure

Your garden is exposed to wind, heat, cold and rain, and some plants are better adapted than others to withstand the potential damage of these forces. Buildings, walls, fences, hills, hedges, trees and even tall perennials influence and often reduce exposure.

Wind and heat are the most likely elements to cause damage. The sun can be very intense, and heat can rise quickly on a sunny afternoon. Choose vegetables that tolerate or even thrive in hot weather for your garden's hot spots.

Too much rain can damage plants, as can over-watering. Early in the season, a light mulch will help prevent seeds or seedlings from being washed away in heavy rain. Later, most established plants beaten down by heavy rain will recover, but some are slow to do so. Waterlogged soil can encourage root rot because many vegetable plants prefer well-drained soil.

Hanging moss-lined baskets are very susceptible to wind and heat overexposure because they lose water from the soil surface and the leaves. Hanging baskets look wonderful, but watch for wilting, and water the baskets regularly to keep them looking great. New water-holding polymers that hold water and release it as the soil dries have been developed for use in soil mixes.

A fence will often reduce exposure.

Frost Tolerance

When choosing vegetables, consider their ability to tolerate an unexpected frost. Most gardeners in Ontario can expect a chance of frost until mid- to late May, though warmer areas may have a last frost date in April and colder areas in June. The map on page 9 gives a general idea of when you can expect your last frost date. Your local garden centre should be able to provide more precise information on frost expectations for your area.

Plants are grouped into three categories based on how tolerant they are of cold weather: hardy, half-hardy or tender.

Hardy plants can tolerate low temperatures and even frost. They can be planted in the garden early and may survive long into fall or even winter, but these plants often fade in the heat of summer after producing an early crop. Many hardy vegetable plants are sown directly in the garden in the weeks before the last frost date, are harvested in early summer, and can be sown again in late summer for a fall crop.

Half-hardy plants can tolerate a light frost but will be killed by a heavy one. These vegetables can be planted out around the last frost date and will generally benefit from being started indoors from seed if they are slow to mature.

Tender plants have no frost tolerance at all and might suffer even if temperatures drop to a few degrees above freezing. These plants are often started early indoors and are not planted out in the garden until the last frost date has passed and the ground has had a chance to warm up. The advantage is that these vegetables are often tolerant of hot summer temperatures.

Eggplants are tender annuals that will do best in the warmest spot in your garden.

Protecting plants from frost is relatively simple. Cover plants overnight with sheets, towels, burlap or even cardboard boxes. Do not use plastic because it doesn't provide any insulation; in fact, it may even trap the cold air and condensation so that you may actually harm the plants you're trying to protect.

Preparing the Garden

Taking the time to properly prepare your garden beds will save you time and effort throughout summer. Starting out with as few weeds as possible and with well-prepared soil that has had organic material added will give your vegetables a good start. For container gardens, use potting soil because regular garden soil loses its structure when used in pots, quickly compacting into a solid mass that drains poorly, and one that doesn't allow for adequate root movement and air circulation.

Organic matter is a small but important component of soil. It increases the water-holding and nutrient-holding capacity of sandy soil and binds together the large particles. In a clay soil, organic matter will increase the water-absorbing and draining potential by opening up spaces between the tiny particles. It will also add the most important element for an organic vegetable garden: micronutrients and micro-organisms. Without these, your plants will become reliant on synthetic fertilizers rather than the beneficial components naturally found in healthy soil. Common organic additives for your soil

Lots of earthworms indicate healthy soil.

include grass clippings, shredded leaves, peat moss, chopped straw and well-rotted manure.

The best evidence of a healthy soil is one filled with fat earthworms. Beyond earthworms is a vast array of life including insects, mites, spiders and various microorganisms, all of which aid plant life by helping to decay organic material and adding structure to the soil. Soil microorganisms live in the rhizosphere, directly adjacent to plant roots. This zone of the soil contains elements, such as sloughed root cells, that provide nutrients for the microorganisms, most of which are capable of developing a symbiotic network with the plant when mutually beneficial relationships develop between the organisms. Some of the beneficial microorganisms in the soil include bacteria, fungi and nematodes. Just 5 millilitres of soil can contain up

to 20,000 different species of microorganisms and up to 2 kilometres of microscopic fungal threads.

Most of these organisms are present in most soils, but enrichment will only benefit your plants. You can amend your soil with such things as compost, worm castings and manure; regular amendments are best. Adding this type of organic matter not only adds to the mix of microorganisms already in the soil but also supports the ones that were already there. Commercial mixtures containing naturally occurring biological agents are slowly becoming available in the marketplace, to farmers and gardeners alike.

Before you plant, loosen the soil with a large garden fork and remove the weeds. Avoid working the soil when it is very wet or very dry because you will damage the soil structure by breaking down the pockets that hold air and water. Add good quality compost and work it into the soil with a spade or fork. To determine how much compost you need, measure the area of your garden and then calculate how much compost you would need to cover it with 5–10 centimetres of compost.

Compost

Compost in an organic vegetable garden is the second most important element for success, secondary only to a live soil. Any organic matter you add to your garden will be of greater benefit to the soil if it has been composted first. In natural environments, compost is created when leaves, plant bits and other debris are broken down on the soil surface. This process will also take place in your garden beds if you work fresh organic matter into the soil. However, the microorganisms

that break down organic matter use the same nutrients as your plants. The tougher the organic matter, the more nutrients in the soil will be used trying to break the matter down, thus robbing your plants of vital nutrients, particularly nitrogen. Also, fresh organic matter and garden debris might encourage or introduce pests and diseases to your garden.

A compost pile or bin, which can be built or purchased, creates a controlled environment where organic matter can be fully broken down before being added to your soil. Good composting methods also reduce the possibility of spreading pests and diseases.

Creating compost is a simple process. Fruit and vegetable kitchen scraps, grass clippings and fall leaves will slowly break down if left in a pile. You can speed up the process by following a few simple guidelines.

An assortment of compost bins

Put both dry and fresh materials into your compost pile, with a larger proportion of dry matter such as chopped straw, shredded leaves and sawdust. Fresh green matter, such as vegetable scraps, grass clippings and pulled weeds, breaks down quickly and produces nitrogen, which feeds the decomposer organisms while they break down the tougher dry matter.

Layer the green matter with the dry matter, and mix in small amounts of previously finished compost or soil from your garden to introduce beneficial microorganisms. If the pile seems very dry, sprinkle on some water. The compost should be moist but not soaking wet, like a wrung-out sponge.

Every week or two, turn the pile over or poke holes into it. Aerating the material will speed up decomposition. A compost pile that is kept aerated can generate a lot of heat. Temperatures can reach 70° C or higher. Such high temperatures destroy weed seeds and kill many damaging organisms. Most beneficial organisms are not killed until the temperature rises higher than 70° C. To monitor the temperature of the compost near the middle of the pile, you will need a thermometer attached to a long probe, similar to a large meat thermometer. Turning your compost when the temperature reaches 70° C will prevent the pile from becoming hot enough to kill the beneficial organisms while stimulating the heating process to begin again.

Don't put diseased or pest-ridden materials into your compost pile.

Suitable materials for compost

If the damaging organisms are not destroyed during the heating process, they could spread throughout your garden.

When you can no longer recognize the matter that you put into the compost pile, and the temperature no longer rises upon turning, your compost is ready to be mixed into your garden beds. Getting to this point can take as little as one month and will leave you with organic material that is rich in nutrients and beneficial organisms.

For gardeners without the space to compost, compost can also be purchased from most garden centres.

Selecting Vegetable Plants

Many gardeners consider the trip to the local garden centre to pick out plants an important rite of spring, and many garden centres offer a few basic vegetable plants, while other retailers offer a diverse selection of harder to find vegetables, particularly as growing edibles regains the popularity it once had. Now you have to decide: do I want to buy my own transplants or seedlings, or do I want to start them myself by seed?

Both methods have benefits, so you might want to use a combination of the two. Purchasing plants provides you with plants that are well grown, which is useful if you don't have the room or the facilities to start seeds. Transplants are more expensive but much less labour intensive than seeds, and more immediate. Growing vegetables from seed will require more time, space and effort—some seeds require specific conditions that are difficult to achieve in a house, or they have erratic germination rates, which makes starting them yourself impractical—but starting from seed offers you a far greater selection of species and varieties because seed catalogues often list many more plants than are offered at garden centres. It's fun and rewarding to know that you grew your food from scratch, but if growing plants from seed is new to you, then you might want to start with only a few seeds, just in case first attempts prove fruitless, so to speak. Starting from seed is discussed starting on page 30.

When browsing through a catalogue, you may find references to hybrid and heirloom seeds. Hybrids are generally newer selections of plants. They have been bred for specific traits such as flavour, size, disease resistance or improved storability. Often developed for market growers and food exporters, hybrids usually have traits that make them suitable for packing

Garden centres have the knowledge and facilities to give plants a good start.

and transporting long distances without spoiling. Many hybrids have also become favourites amongst home gardeners since their introduction. Hybrids rarely come true to type from collected seed.

Heirlooms are plant selections that have been in cultivation for generations. Many gardeners like the connection with history, knowing that their grandparents grew the same plant. Some of the most intriguing vegetable selections are heirlooms, and many advocates claim the vegetables to be among the tastiest and most pest and disease resistant. Seeds can be collected from the plants, and offspring will be true to type.

Purchased plants are grown in a variety of containers. Some are sold in individual pots, some in divided cell-packs and others in undivided trays. Each type has advantages and disadvantages.

Plants in individual pots are usually well established and generally have plenty of space for root growth. These plants have probably been seeded in flat trays and then transplanted into individual pots once they developed a few leaves. The cost of labour, pots and soil can make this option quite expensive.

Plants grown in cell-packs are often inexpensive and hold several plants, making them easy to transport. There is less damage to the roots of the plants when they are transplanted, but because each cell is quite small, it doesn't take too long for a plant to become root-bound.

Plants grown in undivided trays are inexpensive and have plenty of room for root growth and can be left in the trays for longer than other types of containers, but their roots tend to become entangled, making the plants difficult to separate.

Regardless of the type of container, check for roots emerging from the holes at the bottom of the cells, or gently remove the plant from the container to look at the roots. If there are too many roots, the plant

Many gardeners purchase tomato seedlings rather than start the seeds early indoors themselves.

is too mature for the container, especially if the roots are wrapped around the inside of the container in a thick web. Such plants are slow to establish once they are transplanted into the garden.

The plants should be compact and have good colour. Healthy leaves look firm and vibrant. Unhealthy leaves may be wilted, chewed or discoloured. Tall, leggy plants have likely been deprived of light. Check the plants for any signs of insects or diseases. Sickly plants may not survive being transplanted and may spread any pests or diseases they are carrying.

The rootball of a root-bound plant (above)

An unhealthy plant next to a healthy plant (below)

Ensure that you know what type of conditions the transplants prefer, how much space they need and so on. Often this information is on the tag in the container, but if not, question the staff for details. If that is a bust, and you still really want the plant, then do the research to ensure you have what the plant needs to thrive and produce.

Lastly, make sure the plants are moist when leaving the store, particularly if it's a hot day and you're not going directly home. A dry plant in a hot car will only lead to heartbreak. Once you get your plants home, water them if they are dry. Plants growing in small containers may require water more than once a day.

Begin to harden off the plants so they can be transplanted into the garden as soon as possible. Your plants are probably accustomed to growing in the sheltered environment of a greenhouse, and they will need to become accustomed to the climate outdoors. Placing them outdoors in a lightly shaded spot each day and bringing them into a sheltered porch, garage or house each night for about a week will acclimate them to your garden.

Starting Vegetables from Seed

Dozens of catalogues from different growers offer vegetable plants that you can start from seed. Many gardeners spend their chilly winter evenings poring through seed catalogues and planning their spring and summer gardens. Other places to find seeds include the internet, local garden centres and seed exchange groups.

Starting your own plants can save you money, particularly if you need a lot of plants. The basic equipment is not expensive, and most seeds can be started in a sunny window. However, although one or two trays don't take up too much space, you may run out of room if you start more than that. Many gardeners start a few specialty plants themselves but buy most of their plants from a garden centre.

Each plant in this book has specific information on starting it from seed, if any is required, but a few basic steps can be followed for all seeds. The easiest way for the home gardener to start seeds is in cell-packs in trays with plastic dome covers. The cell-packs keep roots separated, and the tray and dome keep moisture in. Seeds can also be started in pots, peat pots or peat pellets. The advantage to starting in peat pots or pellets is that you will not disturb the roots when you transplant the vegetables outside.

Use a growing mix (soil mix) that is intended for seedlings. These mixes are very fine and are usually made from peat moss, vermiculite and perlite. The mix will have good water-holding capacity and will have been sterilized to prevent pests and diseases from attacking your seedlings. One problem that can be caused by soil-borne fungi is called damping off. The affected seedling will appear to have been pinched at soil level. The pinched area blackens and the seedling topples over and dies. Using sterile soil mix, keeping the soil evenly moist and maintaining good air circulation will prevent plants from damping off.

Fill your pots or seed trays with the soil mix and firm it down slightly. Soil that is too firmly packed will not drain well. Moisten the soil before planting your seeds to prevent them from getting washed around. Large seeds can be planted one or two to a cell, but place smaller seeds in a folded piece of paper and sprinkle them evenly over the soil surface. Very tiny seeds can be mixed with fine sand and then sprinkled on the soil surface.

Small seeds do not need to be covered with any more soil, but medium-sized seeds can be lightly covered, and large seeds can be poked into the soil. Some seeds need to be exposed to light to germinate; these ones should be left on the soil surface regardless of their size.

Seed starting supplies

Pot up well-developed seedlings until they can be planted outside.

Place pots or flats of seeds in plastic bags to retain humidity while the seeds are germinating. Many planting trays come with clear plastic covers that keep in the moisture. Remove the plastic once the seeds have germinated.

Water seeds and small seedlings gently with a fine spray from a hand-held mister—small seeds can easily be washed around if the spray is too strong. Water all newly seeded plants gently, particularly those that are not covered in soil, potting mix or other medium, and those that are incredibly tiny, or you'll find them growing everywhere they travelled to when they were washed or blown away.

Seeds provide all the energy and nutrients that young seedlings require. Small seedlings do not need to be fertilized until they have about four or five true leaves. When the first leaves that sprouted begin to shrivel, the plant has used up all its seed energy, and you can begin to use a fertilizer diluted to quarter strength.

If the seedlings get too big for their containers before you are ready to plant them outside, you may have to "up-pot" them to prevent them from becoming root-bound. Harden plants off by exposing them to outdoor conditions for longer every day for at least a week before planting them out.

Some seeds can be planted directly in the garden. The procedure is similar to that of starting seeds indoors. Begin with a well-prepared bed that has been smoothly raked. The small furrows left by the rake help hold moisture and prevent the seeds from being washed away. Sprinkle the seeds onto the soil and cover them lightly with peat moss or more soil. Larger seeds can be planted slightly deeper. Very tiny seeds should be mixed with sand for more even sowing. The soil should be kept moist to ensure even germination. Use a gentle spray to avoid washing the seeds around the bed because they inevitably pool into dense clumps. Cover your newly seeded bed with chicken wire, an old sheet or some thorny branches to discourage pets from digging it up.

Larger seeds are easy to space out an appropriate distance from each other when you sow them. With smaller seeds, you may find that the new plants need to be thinned out to give adjacent plants room to grow properly. Pull out the weaker plants when groups look crowded. Some are edible and can be used as spring greens in a salad or steamed as a side dish.

Growing Vegetables

In Ontario, most vegetables are grown throughout the growing season, from spring thaw to the first killing frosts in fall. There are exceptions, of course, but the perennial vegetable plants are in the minority. Growing vegetables is incredibly rewarding because the end result is delicious and nutritious food for our families. There is a feeling of satisfaction when you can make a contribution to your family's food security and overall health, but growing your own vegetables will also help the environment by making a contribution toward sustainable, local food production. For a bit of physical labour, and very little cost or time, you could be harvesting from spring to fall—in a few parts of the province, almost year-round—and here's how.

Planting

Once your plants have hardened off, it is time to plant them out. If your beds are already prepared, you are ready to start. The only tool you are likely to need is a trowel. Be sure you set aside enough time to do the job. You don't want to have young plants out of their pots and not finish planting them. If they are left out in the sun, they can quickly dry out and die. To help avoid this problem, choose an overcast or cool day for planting. Do not plant in the middle of the day when it's scorching hot.

Plants are easier to remove from their containers if the soil is moist. Push on the bottom of the cell or pot with your thumb to ease the plants out. If the plants were growing in an undivided tray, you will

When you're ready to plant, the only tool you'll need is a trowel.

have to gently untangle the roots. If the roots are very tangled, immerse them in water and wash some of the soil away. This should free the plants from one another. If you must handle a plant, hold it by a leaf to avoid crushing the stem. Remove and discard any damaged leaves or growth.

The rootball should contain a network of white plant roots. If the rootball is densely matted and twisted, break the tangles apart with your thumbs to encourage the roots to extend and grow outward. New root growth will start from the breaks, allowing the plant to spread outward.

Plants started in peat pots and peat pellets can be planted pot and all. When planting peat pots into the garden, remove the top 4 to 6 centimetres of pot. If any of the pot is sticking up out of the soil, it can wick moisture away from your plant.

Use your trowel to make a planting hole.

Holding the plant in one hand, insert your trowel or your opposite hand into the soil and pull it toward you, creating a wedge. Place your plant into the hole and firm the soil around it with your hands. Water gently but thoroughly. Until it is established, the plant will need regular watering.

Some of the plants in this book are sold in relatively large containers. Plants in large containers can be planted as described above, except that they may require larger holes than the wedge a trowel makes. In a prepared bed, dig a hole that will accommodate the rootball. Fill the hole in gradually, settling the soil with water as you go.

Other vegetables may be sold as bare roots or crowns, or in moistened peat moss, sphagnum moss or sawdust. Plants that are sold without soil should be soaked in water for a few hours before planting as above, again being sure to accommodate the roots.

A few vegetables, such as garlic and onion sets, are sold as bulbs, which can be planted about three times as deep as the bulb is high.

More detailed planting instructions are given, as needed, in the plant accounts.

Mulching

Use a mulch to cover exposed soil between your vegetables; the benefits of doing so will be endless. A layer of mulch around your plants prevents light from reaching weed seeds, keeping them from germinating. Those that do germinate will be smothered or will be unable to reach the surface, exhausting their energy before getting a chance to grow. Mulch also helps maintain consistent soil temperatures and effectively retains moisture. In areas that receive heavy wind or rainfall, mulch protects the soil and prevents erosion. Plus, organic mulches such as compost, grass clippings or shredded leaves add nutrients to the soil as they break down, thus improving the quality of the soil and, ultimately, the health of your plants.

Layer the mulch 5 to 10 centimetres thick over the soil after you have finished planting, or spread your mulch first and then make spaces to plant afterward. Water it in and leave it for about a week so it can settle undisturbed. Make sure it is not piled too thickly around the crowns and stems of your plants. Mulch that is too close to plants traps moisture, prevents air circulation and encourages fungal disease. Replenish your mulch as it breaks down over summer, and annually sprinkle a thin layer of compost over the mulch and water it in. If the mulch you applied is of an acidic nature, such as ground conifers, then you might also want to apply a thin dusting of dolomite lime to reduce any acidity in the soil.

Underneath this glorious mulch, the earthworms do their job by aerating the soil and producing a product that is priceless to the soil and your plants. They will also do the job of pulling the nutrients from the compost and decomposing mulch further down in the soil around the root zone of the plants, leaving you with more time to enjoy the fruits of your labour, rather than continuing to toil away.

Weeding

Weeds are a symptom of an unbalanced landscape, whether it be a vegetable garden or a parking lot. They are also a symptom of disturbance. I like to think of weeds as plants that may be in the wrong location, or plants we simply have not found a use for yet. This kinder perception calms my sense of wanting to control weeds, and it helps me to have a better understanding of why they're there and how I can better maintain a balance in that location, using gentle methods. If more people looked upon weeds this way, there would be far fewer synthetic herbicides in our environment.

A straw mulch is of benefit to these soybeans.

Weeds are not all bad. Some provide benefits to the garden. Deeply rooted weeds bring nutrients to the surface, making them available for your vegetable plants, and help to aerate the soil and prevent soil erosion. Many weeds are sources of food for beneficial insects. Clover, milkweed, nettles, thistles, chickweed, wild mustard and Queen Anne's lace are all attractive to organisms that will benefit your garden.

Clover can be beneficial, so leave it alone unless it begins to crowd out the squash.

One tip for weed prevention is to not bring weeds into your garden, either in newly purchased transplants, on your shoes or on your tools. Make sure your tools are clean before using them in the garden.

There are highly aggressive plants that can easily take over your garden, and these invasive weeds may require eradication. Other weeds are only creeping into landscapes and spaces that we have created, doing what they were meant to do: repairing the damage from soil disturbances and erosion; providing forage for millions of insects globally, some of which are pollinators including butterflies and bees; acting as a live mulch around other existing plants; and providing food for animals, and even for humans—at least, for the lucky ones who know what to do with the weeds. There are many valuable uses for plants we consider to be weeds. We all need to be educated and reminded of their value.

So what do you do with the weeds in your garden? First, accept that they are part of the landscape. Then use organic, safe methods of eradication, to a point, as well as gentle measures to prevent them from growing in the first place. Pull weeds by hand or with a hoe. The easiest time to pull them will be shortly after a rainfall, when the soil is soft and damp. A hoe scuffed quickly across the soil surface will uproot small weeds and sever large ones from their roots. Try to pull out weeds while they are still small. Certainly having some weeds in your garden isn't the end of the world, but once they are large enough to flower, many will quickly set seed; then you will have a whole new generation to worry about.

It can be a little daunting to witness the vigour and aggressiveness of weeds. We've all been there, cussing at all of the weeds that have taken over our well-tilled garden spaces. The first step in weed prevention is understanding how weeds start in the first place. Millions of seeds are present in the soil, aside from the ones that blow in from other locations. The seeds in the soil are able to produce an annual crop for a minimum of nine years, and longer for the more persistent species. All they require to germinate is light. Every time the soil is disturbed, be it from digging, tilling or even walking on it, more seeds are exposed and the germination rate is increased exponentially. Adapt by turning the garden as little as possible. Instead, use a deep-dig method by preparing the garden soil more thoroughly at the beginning. Only the topsoil should be dug thoroughly and broken up into smaller pieces, followed by additions of compost and other soil amendments. Then comes resisting the temptation to dig, hoe and till time and time again to reduce the weed population, when in fact you're only encouraging it.

Watering

Water thoroughly but infrequently. Plants given a light sprinkle of water every day develop roots that stay close to the soil surface, making the plants vulnerable to heat and dry spells. Plants given a deep watering once a week develop a deeper root system. In a dry spell, they will be adapted to seeking out water trapped deep in the ground.

This rule applies to established or rooted plants only, not to seeds, young seedlings or newly transplanted plants. Seeds need to be kept consistently moist while germinating and rooting, and seedlings and newly transplanted plants need consistent moisture as their root systems become established. Once they're rooted in and of a size that they can go for longer periods without supplemental water, then you can water

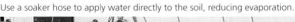
Use a soaker hose to apply water directly to the soil, reducing evaporation.

more deeply and less frequently. Use mulch to prevent water from evaporating out of the soil.

Be sure the water penetrates at least 10 centimetres into the soil; this is approximately 2.5 centimetres of applied water. To save time, money and water, you may wish to install an irrigation system, which applies the water exactly where it is needed: near the roots. Drip irrigation is as simple as a soaker hose set on the soil among the plants and hooked up to a water source. A timer can also be applied for regular, measured watering. A drip system has several advantages:

- quantity of water used is much less than with conventional methods

- moisture is applied almost directly to the roots, slowly, resulting in better penetration

- the soil is watered more evenly and thoroughly

- less effort is spent in moving hoses and equipment because you do it less often.

Consult with your local garden centre or landscape professionals for more information.

Plants in hanging baskets and planters will probably need to be watered more frequently than plants in the ground—even twice daily during hot, sunny weather. The smaller the container, the more often the plants need watering.

The best time to water is always early in the morning, whether it's manually, by sprinkler or by soaker hose. The plants then have time to dry off before the sun is at its hottest, while the moist soil keeps them cool for as long as possible into the day. Early morning watering also reduces evaporation, which results in less water used and wasted.

Fertilizing

We demand a lot of growth and production from many of our vegetable plants; annual ones in particular are expected to grow to maturity and provide us with a good crop of vegetables, all in one growing season. They, in return, demand a lot of sun, water and nutrients. Mixing plenty of compost into the soil is a good start, but fertilizing regularly can make a big difference when it comes time to harvest your crop.

First and foremost, for an organic garden, use organic and natural (not synthetic) fertilizers because they are non-toxic and will not harm the microorganisms in the soil. Natural fertilizers are also generally less concentrated and less likely to burn the roots of your plants, and they often improve the soil as they feed your plants. Your local garden centre should carry organic fertilizers, or you can make your own at home, even if you live in an apartment or condominium.

When using packaged fertilizers, particularly concentrates, follow the directions very carefully. Using too much fertilizer can harm or kill your plants by burning their roots, and it may upset the microbial balance of your soil, allowing pathogens to move in or dominate. Regardless of whether you use a natural or synthetic fertilizer, too much is never better.

There are many naturally sourced, safe, non-toxic fertilizers on the market today. Based on my experiences, particularly in regard to growing edible plants, I recommend the following: fish fertilizers, rock dusts, compost, composted manure and compost tea, which you can make at home.

Compost tea aids in suppressing diseases that can affect your vegetable plants.

Compost or manure tea is one of the easiest and best forms of fertilizer you can use. Simply put well-composted manure or compost into a burlap sack or old pillow case, tie at the top, attach to a strong stick or rod and dunk into a vessel of rainwater (treated water can be used but needs to be left for a day or two in the sun for the chemicals to dissipate before adding the living compost). Let it steep for a couple of hours to days (hours is better because the microbe population starts decreasing if left too long, and you will want to use the tea when it has the highest microbe count), and you will have a fertilizer concentrate. The tea, if super fresh, can be used immediately and without diluting, either as a foliar spray or as a drench simply by pouring it into the soil where the plants are growing. When steeped for longer periods, such as a day or two, it is best to dilute it by half before using it to water your plants. You can apply the tea weekly, or as infrequently as monthly. For foliar disease prevention, spray the plants just before you would usually have the onset of disease occurring. Then spray every 10 to 14 days for about a month.

Making compost tea (all below)

Extending the Growing Season

Frost is often the almighty threat we face as gardeners. It determines whether the season will continue or not. However, there are ways to protect plants to extend your growing season by days, weeks, even months, depending on the route you take. Methods include cold frames, cloches and greenhouses.

Cold air tends to move downward to the lowest point, following the slopes in hills, walls and so on. The cool air will pool around anything that prevents it from moving any farther, such as a grouping of plants or a structure. Plants are better prepared to ward off any exposure to that cold air or to frost if they've been hardened off. Harden off your plants started indoors by gradually acclimating them to outside conditions by setting them in a sheltered location outdoors for increasing lengths of time over a period of days.

Cold frames are used to protect young plants grown from seeds or cuttings. A cold frame is a small wooden structure with a slanted glass or plexi-glass lid, often built very close to the ground, that acts like a mini greenhouse by allowing the light to penetrate for plant growth and to heat the inside of the structure. The top is built to open fully for access to the plants, but it can also be opened just slightly throughout the day to prevent the plants from becoming too warm and to slowly harden off the plants inside to the temperatures outside.

Cloches serve the same purpose as cold frames and can be lifted slightly on one side during the day, allowing

Use a cold frame to protect seedlings.

the plant to gradually acclimate to the surrounding air temperatures, but whereas cold frames protect groups of plants, cloches are for individual plants. They are often bell-shaped and made of blown, thickened glass for longevity, but I've also seen plastic versions that are much less expensive and easier to store. A great resource for the construction of cloches is the plastic bottle; simply cut the bottom from a plastic water or pop bottle and place the bottle over top of the seedling. The lid can be left on at night and removed during the day, allowing the air to move freely in and out while the plant acclimates to outside temperatures. Later on the neck of the bottle can be cut away, leaving only a plastic cylinder around the base of the plant to protect it from chewing insects as well as to act as a support throughout the growing season. Or the bottle can be taken away all together.

Greenhouses are of course a world unto their own. If you want one, there are fantastic resources in your local library, book store, horticultural extension of your university or college, garden centre or greenhouse builder. The work and expense is well worth the end result. With a greenhouse, regardless of size, you can extend your season by weeks or months, or you can just garden year-round. A greenhouse provides the best protection from the outdoor elements and is invaluable to gardeners in regions with short summers and cold winters. Plants can be raised from seed to maturity, regardless of the time of year, or they can be started in the greenhouse and moved to cold frames before they're planted outdoors for the duration of the growing season.

Harvesting

Each plant featured in this book will have suggestions of when to harvest, but here are a few general tips.

Make a list of the maturity dates for the vegetable plants you're growing. Once the time allowance has been met, observe the vegetables to see if they're ready to be harvested. Don't harvest too early or too late. Vegetables picked earlier than necessary are

To enjoy corn at its best, don't pick it too early or too late.

often bland, hard and small. Veggies that are left too long are often bland, tough and stringy. Only trial and error will teach you when the perfect time to harvest is, but observe and taste your produce and record your findings to better prepare for the following growing season.

The window of opportunity for some leafy vegetables, such as lettuce, spinach, arugula and mustard greens, is small. Pick them early in the season or they become bitter and unusable, and pick just the amount you need for one sitting, rather than picking them all at once. Once they're past their prime, pull them up and re-seed for an additional crop.

For the best culinary experience, try to harvest right before preparing, cooking or eating the produce to get the full benefit of the flavour and nutrients. However, if you're planning on storing the produce, particularly leafy vegetables, for any length of time, harvest early in the morning, preferably a cool morning when dew is left behind on the leaves.

Use sharp, clean tools when harvesting vegetables. Some plants can be damaged when the fruit is pulled off rather than cut off with a sharp tool, which may result in a plant that is no longer able to produce. Pulling on a tomato and snapping your tomato plant in half early on will be the season's biggest disappointment, particularly since it could have been prevented.

There are many more tips and tricks to learn that will help you, not only throughout the growing phase of vegetables but during the harvest as well. The foregoing are only the basics. Strike up a conversation with friends, family and neighbours who garden, and you'll soon find that some of their tried-and-true methods will become part of your seasonal routine.

Harvesting throughout the season is the best reward for all of your hard work.

Guide to Pests and Diseases

Most vegetable plants are planted new each spring and may be a different species each year. These factors make it difficult for pests and diseases to find their preferred host plants and establish a population. However, many vegetables are closely related, and any problems that set in over summer are likely to attack all the plants in the same family.

For many years, pest control meant spraying or dusting with the goal to eliminate every pest in the landscape. A more moderate approach advocated today is IPM: Integrated Pest (or Plant) Management. The goal of IPM is to reduce pest problems so only negligible damage is done. Of course, you must determine what degree of damage is acceptable to you. Consider whether a pest's damage is localized or covers the entire plant. Will the damage kill the plant or is it only affecting the outward appearance? Are there methods of controlling the pest without chemicals?

A good IPM program includes learning about your plants and the conditions they need for healthy growth, which pests might affect your plants, where and when to look for those pests and how to control them. Keep records of pest damage because your observations can reveal patterns useful in spotting recurring problems and in planning your maintenance regime.

There are four steps in effective and responsible pest management. Cultural controls are the most important and are the first response when

All plants in the Brassica family, including Brussels sprouts, are somewhat prone to pests and diseases.

problems arise. Physical controls should be attempted next, followed by biological controls. Resort to chemical controls only when the first three possibilities have been completely exhausted, and even then, consider that there may be alternatives you're not aware of. It's worth it to do a little research before applying a synthetic, chemical pesticide; to use one will disrupt the organic garden, rendering it non-organic.

Cultural controls are the gardening techniques you use in the day-to-day care of your garden. Keeping your plants as healthy as possible is the best defence against pests. Growing plants in the conditions they prefer and keeping your soil healthy by adding plenty of organic matter are just two of the cultural controls you can use to keep pests manageable. Choose problem-resistant varieties of plants. Space the plants so that they have good air circulation around them and are not stressed by competing for light, nutrients and space. Take plants that are decimated by the same pests every year out of the landscape. Remove diseased foliage and burn it or take it to a permitted dumpsite. Prevent the spread of disease by keeping gardening tools clean and by tidying up fallen leaves and dead plant matter at the end of every growing season.

Physical controls are generally used to combat pest problems: picking insects off plants by hand, erecting barriers that stop pests from getting to the plants, and setting up traps that catch or confuse pests. Physical control of disease often necessitates removing the infected plant part or parts to prevent the spread of the problem.

Biological controls use predators that prey on pests. Animals such as birds, snakes, frogs, spiders and lady beetles, as well as certain bacteria, can play an important role in keeping pest populations manageable. Encourage these creatures to take up permanent residence in your garden. A birdbath and birdfeeder will

Lady beetle larva

Lady beetle

encourage birds to enjoy your yard and feed on a wide variety of insect pests. Many beneficial insects are probably already living in your landscape, and you can encourage them to stay by planting appropriate food sources. Many beneficial insects eat nectar from flowers such as coriander and perennial yarrow.

Chemical controls should be rarely necessary, but if you absolutely must use them, there are some organic options available. Organic sprays are no less dangerous than synthetic ones, but they break down into harmless compounds. The main drawback to using any chemicals is that they may also kill the beneficial

Use IPM techniques to maintain a healthy garden.

insects you have been trying to attract to your garden. Organic chemicals are available at most garden centres.

Follow the manufacturer's instructions carefully. A large amount of pesticide is not going to be any more effective in controlling pests than the recommended amount. Note that if a particular pest is not listed on the package, that product will not control that pest. Proper and early identification of pests is vital to finding a quick solution.

Whereas cultural, physical, biological and chemical controls are all possible defences against insects, diseases must be controlled culturally. It is usually weakened plants that succumb to diseases. Healthy plants can often fight off illness, though some diseases can infect plants regardless of their level of health. Prevention is often the only hope; once a plant has been infected,

it should probably be destroyed to prevent the disease from spreading.

The Pests and Diseases

Anthracnose

Fungus. Yellow or brown spots on leaves; sunken lesions and blisters on stems; can kill plant.

What to do: choose resistant varieties and cultivars; keep soil well drained; thin out stems to improve air circulation; avoid handling wet foliage; remove and destroy infected plant parts; clean up and destroy debris from infected plants at end of growing season.

Aphids

Insects; e.g., woolly adelgids. Tiny, pear-shaped, green, black, brown, red or grey; can be winged or wingless. Cluster along stems, on buds and on leaves; suck sap from plant; cause

Aphids

distorted or stunted growth; sticky honeydew forms on plant surfaces and encourages sooty mould growth.

What to do: squish small colonies by hand; dislodge with brisk water spray; encourage predatory insects and birds that feed on aphids; spray serious infestations with insecticidal soap or neem oil according to package directions.

Aster Yellows

see Viruses

Beetles

Insects; many types. Usually rounded with hard, shell-like outer wings covering membranous inner wings; vary in size. Some are beneficial, e.g., ladybird beetles ("ladybugs"); others, e.g., Japanese beetles, leaf skeletonizers and weevils, eat plants. Leave wide range of chewing damage: make small or large holes in or around margins of leaves; consume entire leaves or areas between leaf veins ("skeletonize"); may also chew holes in flowers. Some bark beetle species carry deadly plant diseases. Larvae: *see* Borers; Grubs.

What to do: pick beetles off at night and drop them into an old coffee can half filled with soapy water (soap prevents them from floating and climbing out).

Blight

Fungal diseases; many types, e.g., leaf blight, needle blight, snow blight. Leaves, stems and flowers blacken, rot and die.

What to do: remove and destroy infected plant parts; thin stems to improve air circulation; keep mulch away from base of plants; remove debris from garden at end of growing season.

Colorado potato beetle

Borers

Larvae of some moths, wasps and beetles; among the most damaging plant pests. Worm-like; vary in size and get bigger as they bore through plants. Burrow into plant stems, branches, leaves and/or roots; destroy vascular tissue (plant veins and arteries) and structural strength. May see tunnels in leaves, stems or roots; stems weaken and may break; leaves will wilt; rhizomes may be hollowed out entirely or in part.

What to do: may be able to squish borers within leaves; remove and destroy bored parts; may need to dig up and destroy infected roots and rhizomes.

Bugs (True Bugs)

Insects; many are beneficial, but a few are pests. Green, brown, black or brightly coloured and patterned; up to 13 mm long. Pierce plants to suck out sap; toxins may be injected that deform plants. Sunken areas remain where pierced; leaves rip as they grow; leaves, buds and new growth may be dwarfed and deformed.

What to do: remove debris and weeds from around plants in fall to destroy overwintering sites. Spray plants with insecticidal soap or neem oil according to package directions.

Case Bearers

see Caterpillars

Caterpillars

Larvae of butterflies, moths and sawflies; include bagworms, budworms, case bearers, cutworms, leaf rollers, leaf tiers, loopers. Chew

Borer damage

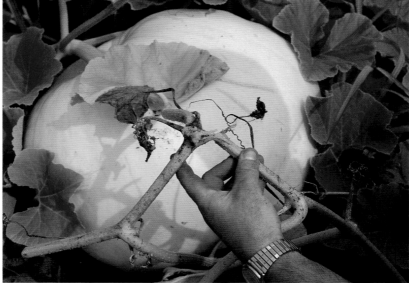

foliage and buds; can completely defoliate a plant if infestation is severe.

What to do: removal from plant is best control; use high-pressure water and soap or pick caterpillars off by hand. Control biologically using the naturally occurring soil bacterium *Bacillus thuringiensis* var. *kurstaki* or *B.t.k.* (commercially available), which breaks down the gut lining of caterpillars.

Cutworms

see Caterpillars

Deer

Can decimate crops, woodlands and gardens; can kill saplings by rubbing their antlers on the trees, girdling the bark or snapping the trees in two; host ticks that carry Lyme disease and Rocky Mountain spotted fever.

What to do: many deterrents work for a while: encircle immature shrubs with tall, upright sticks; place dangling soap bars around the garden; use noisemaking devices or water spritzers to startle deer; mount flashy aluminum or moving devices throughout the garden.

Galls

Unusual swellings of plant tissues that may be caused by insects or diseases. Can affect leaves, buds, stems, flowers, fruit; often a specific gall affects a single genus or species.

What to do: cut galls out of plant and destroy them. A gall caused by an insect usually contains the insect's eggs and juvenile stages; prevent such galls by controlling the insect before

Galls

it lays eggs; otherwise try to remove and destroy infected tissue before young insects emerge; insect galls are generally more unsightly than damaging to plant. Galls caused by diseases often require destruction of plant; don't place other plants susceptible to same disease in that location.

Grey Mould

see Blight

Grubs

Larvae of different beetles. White or grey body; head may be white, grey, brown or reddish; usually curled in C-shape; commonly found below soil level. Problematic in lawns; may feed on roots of perennials. Plant wilts despite regular watering; may pull easily out of ground in severe cases.

What to do: toss grubs onto a stone path, driveway, road or patio for birds to devour; apply parasitic nematodes or milky spore to infested soil (ask at your local garden centre).

Leafhoppers and Treehoppers

Insects. Small, wedge-shaped; can be green, brown, grey or multi-coloured; jump around frantically when disturbed. Suck juice from plant leaves; cause distorted growth; carry diseases such as aster yellows.

What to do: encourage predators by planting nectar-producing species such as coriander. Wash insects off with strong spray of water; spray with insecticidal soap or neem oil according to package directions.

Leaf Miners

Larvae of some butterflies and moths. Tiny, stubby; yellow or green. Tunnel within leaves, leaving winding trails; tunnelled areas lighter in colour than

Leaf miner damage

rest of leaf. Unsightly rather than major health risk to plant.

What to do: remove debris from area in fall to destroy overwintering sites; attract parasitic wasps with nectar plants such as yarrow and coriander; remove and destroy infected foliage; can sometimes squish larvae by hand within leaf.

Leaf Rollers

see Caterpillars

Leaf Skeletonizers

see Beetles

Leaf Spot

Two common types: one caused by bacteria, the other by fungi. Bacterial: small brown or purple spots grow to encompass entire leaves; leaves may drop. Fungal: black, brown or yellow spots; leaves wither; e.g., scab, tar spot.

What to do: Bacterial: infection more severe, must remove entire plant. Fungal: remove and destroy infected plant parts; sterilize removal tools; avoid wetting foliage or touching wet foliage; remove and destroy debris at end of growing season.

Maggots

Larvae of several species of flies (cabbage root maggots, carrot rust flies). Small, white or grey; worm-like. Tunnel into roots of a variety of plants, including many root vegetables. Stunt plants and disfigure roots; serious infestations can kill plants.

What to do: use floating row covers to prevent flies from laying eggs near roots. Apply parasitic nematodes to soil around plants. Use an early crop of radishes as a trap crop; pull them up and destroy them as soon as they become infested with maggots.

Mealybugs

Insects; related to aphids. Tiny; appear to be covered with white fuzz or flour. Sucking damage stunts and stresses plant; excrete honeydew that promotes growth of sooty mould.

Root maggots on radishes

Mealybugs

What to do: remove by hand from smaller plants; wash plant with soap and water or wipe with alcohol-soaked swabs; spray with insecticidal soap; remove heavily infested leaves. Encourage or introduce natural predators such as mealybug destroyer beetles and parasitic wasps. Larvae of mealybug destroyer beetles look like very large mealybugs.

Mice

Burrow under mulch in winter, chewing plant roots, bark, bulbs and many other underground goodies; even plants or roots stored in cool porches, garages or sheds are fair game.

What to do: fine wire mesh can prevent mice from getting at your plants in winter, though they are quite ingenious and may find their way through or around any barrier you erect; roll bulbs and lifted roots in talcum powder, garlic powder or bulb protectant spray before storing or planting. Get a cat, or borrow your neighbour's, if you must.

Mildew

Two types, both caused by fungus, but with slightly different symptoms. Downy mildew: yellow spots on upper sides of leaves and downy fuzz on undersides; fuzz may be yellow, white or grey. Powdery mildew: white or grey, powdery coating on leaf surfaces that doesn't brush off.

What to do: choose resistant cultivars; space plants well; thin stems to encourage air circulation; tidy any debris in fall; remove and destroy infected parts.

Powdery mildew

Spider mite web

Mites

Eight-legged relatives of spiders; e.g., bud mites, spider mites, spruce mites. Tiny, almost invisible to naked eye; red, yellow or green. Do not eat insects, but may spin webs; usually found on undersides of plant leaves; may see fine webbing on leaves and stems or mites moving on leaf undersides. Suck juice out of leaves; leaves become discoloured and speckled, then turn brown and shrivel up.

What to do: wash off with strong spray of water daily until all signs of infestation are gone; spray plants with insecticidal soap. Predatory mites are available through garden centres.

Moles and Gophers

Burrow under the soil, tunnelling throughout your property in search of insects, grubs and earthworms; tunnels can create runways for voles that will eat your plants from below ground.

What to do: castor oil (the primary ingredient in most repellents made to thwart moles and gophers) spilled down the mole's runway is effective and is available in granulated pellet form, too; noisemakers and predator urine are also useful; humane trapping is effective, as is having a cat or dog.

Mosaic

see Viruses

Nematodes

Tiny worms that give plants disease symptoms; one type infects foliage and stems, the other infects roots. Foliar: leaves have yellow spots that turn brown; leaves shrivel and wither; problem starts on lowest leaves and works up plant. Root-knot: plant is stunted and may wilt; yellow spots on leaves; roots have tiny bumps or knots.

What to do: mulch soil; add organic matter; clean up debris in fall; don't touch wet foliage of infected plants. Can add parasitic nematodes to soil; remove infected plants in extreme cases.

Rabbits

Can eat as much of your garden as deer and munch on the bark of trees and shrubs.

What to do: deterrents that work for deer usually keep rabbits away, as will humane trapping; having a cat or dog patrol your garden may also be effective.

Raccoons

Are especially fond of fruit and some vegetables; can carry rabies and canine distemper; also eat grubs, insects and mice, so can sometimes be helpful to gardeners.

What to do: don't allow access to garbage or pet food. Humane traps and relocation are best solutions; call your local SPCA or Humane Society to relocate individuals.

Rot

Several different fungi that affect different parts of plant, sometimes even killing it. Crown rot: affects base of plant; stems blacken and fall over; leaves turn yellow and wilt. Root rot: leaves turn yellow and wilt; digging up plant shows roots rotted away. White rot: a "watery decay fungus" that affects any part

Rust

of plant; cell walls appear to break down, releasing fluids.

What to do: keep soil well drained; don't damage plant if you are digging around it; keep mulches away from plant base; destroy infected plant if whole plant is affected.

Rust

Fungi; e.g., blister rust, hollyhock rust. Pale spots on upper leaf surfaces; orange, fuzzy or dusty spots on leaf undersides.

What to do: choose rust-resistant varieties and cultivars; avoid handling wet leaves; provide plant with good air circulation; clear up garden debris at end of season; remove and destroy infected plant parts.

Scab

see Leaf Spot

Scale Insects

Tiny, shelled insects. Suck sap, weakening and possibly killing plant or making it vulnerable to other problems; once female scale insect has pierced plant with mouthpart, it is there for life. Juvenile scale insects are called crawlers.

What to do: wipe bugs off with alcohol-soaked swabs; spray plant with water to dislodge crawlers; prune out heavily infested branches. Encourage natural predators and parasites; spray dormant oil in spring before bud break.

Slugs and Snails

Slugs lack shells; snails have a spiral shell; both have slimy, smooth skin;

Slug (above)

Snail (below)

can be up to 20 cm long but are usually much smaller; grey, green, black, beige, yellow or spotted. Leave large, ragged holes in leaves and silvery slime trails on and around plants.

What to do: attach strips of copper to wood around raised beds or smaller boards inserted around susceptible groups of plants (slugs and snails get shocked if they touch copper surfaces); pick off by hand in evening and squish or drop in a can of soapy water; spread wood ash or diatomaceous earth (available in garden centres) around plants (it pierces their soft bodies and causes them to dehydrate); use slug baits containing iron phosphate. If slugs caused damage last season, begin controls as soon as new green shoots appear in spring.

Sooty Mould

Fungus. Thin, black film forms on leaf surfaces and reduces amount of light getting to leaf surfaces.

What to do: wipe mould off leaves; control aphids, mealybugs and whiteflies (honeydew left on leaves encourages mould).

Squirrels

Unearth and eat bulbs and corms, as well as flowers, fruits and vegetables; hone their teeth on almost everything else; raid birdfeeders and often eat the feeder itself; bury their food for later consumption, which can result in seeds germinating and plants springing up where you never wanted them.

What to do: cut heavy metal screening (hardware cloth) to fit around the plant stem; caging entire plants is effective if you don't mind your garden looking like a zoo; removing enticing food supplies is effective, but often impractical; trapping and moving is one option but usually results in other squirrels moving in.

Squirrel

Tar Spot

see Leaf Spot

Thrips

Insects. Tiny, slender; yellow, black or brown; narrow, fringed wings; difficult to see but may be visible if you disturb them by blowing gently on an infested flower. Suck juice out of plant cells, particularly in flowers and buds; cause mottled petals and leaves, dying buds and distorted and stunted growth.

What to do: remove and destroy infected plant parts; encourage native predatory insects with nectar plants like yarrow or coriander; spray severe infestations with insecticidal soap or neem oil according to package directions.

Viruses

Include aster yellows, mosaic virus and ringspot virus. Plant may be

Mosaic virus

stunted and leaves and flowers distorted, streaked or discoloured.

What to do: viral diseases in plants
cannot be treated. Control disease-
spreading insects, such as aphids,
leafhoppers and whiteflies; destroy
infected plants.

Voles

Mouse-like creatures. Damage
plants at or just beneath the soil
surface; mostly herbivorous, feeding
on a variety of grasses, herbaceous
plants, bulbs (lilies are a favourite)
and tubers; also eat bark and roots

of trees, usually in fall or winter;
store seeds and other plant matter
in underground chambers.

What to do: wire fences at least
30 cm tall with a mesh size of 1 cm
or less and buried 15–20 cm deep
can help exclude voles from gardens;
fence can either stand alone or be
attached to the bottom of an existing fence; a weed-free barrier outside fence will increase effectiveness.
Burrow fumigants do not effectively
control voles because the vole's burrow system is shallow and has many
open holes; electromagnetic or
ultrasonic devices and flooding are

Use a pheremone trap to monitor insect populations.

also ineffective. When vole populations are not numerous or are concentrated in a small area, trapping may be effective; use enough traps to control the population: for a small garden use at least 12 traps, and for larger areas 50 or more may be needed. A dog or cat is a deterrent. Do not use poisonous repellents or baits if your pets or children romp around the garden.

Weevils

see Beetles

Whiteflies

Insects. Tiny, white, moth-like; flutter up into the air when plant is disturbed; live on undersides of plant leaves. Suck juice out of leaves, causing yellowed leaves and weakened plants; leave behind sticky honeydew on leaves, encouraging sooty mould growth.

What to do: destroy weeds where insects may live; attract native predatory beetles and parasitic wasps with nectar plants like yarrow or coriander; spray severe cases with insecticidal soap. Can make a sticky flypaper-like trap by mounting a tin can on a stake, wrapping can with yellow paper and covering it with a clear plastic bag smeared with petroleum jelly; replace bag when covered in flies.

Wilt

If watering doesn't help wilted plants, one of two wilt fungi may be to blame. *Fusarium* wilt: plant wilts; leaves turn yellow then die; symptoms generally appear first on one part of plant before spreading to other parts. *Verticillium* wilt: plant wilts; leaves curl up at edges; leaves turn yellow then drop off; plant may die.

What to do: both wilts are difficult to control; choose resistant plant varieties and cultivars; clean up debris at end of growing season. Destroy infected plants; solarize (sterilize) soil before replanting (may help if entire bed of plants lost to these fungi)—contact local garden centre for assistance.

Woolly Adelgids

see Aphids

Worms

see Caterpillars, Nematodes

Homemade Insecticidal Soap

- ❀ 5 mL (1 tsp) mild dish detergent or pure soap (biodegradeable options are available)
- ❀ 1 litre (4 cups) water

Mix in a clean spray bottle and spray the surface of your plants. Rinse well within an hour to avoid foliage discoloration.

About this Guide

The plants featured in this book are organized alphabetically by their most common familiar names. Additional common names appear as well. This system enables you to find a plant easily if you are familiar with only the common name. The scientific or botanical name is always listed after the common name. I encourage you to learn these botanical names. Several plants may share the same common name, and they vary from region to region. Only the specific botanical name identifies the specific plant anywhere in the world.

Each entry gives clear instructions for planting and growing the plants, and recommends many favourite selections. In reference to spacing while planting or sowing seed, a plant's height and spread ranges are listed as general guidelines, but gardening intensively will reduce space requirements somewhat. All outstanding features are described in the recommended section of each vegetable account, particularly the unusual species, cultivars, hybrids and varieties. Your local garden centre will have any additional information you need about the plant and will help you make your final plant selections.

Following the more traditional vegetable accounts is a grouping of other vegetables to consider, beginning with amaranth. These vegetables are noteworthy because they're not commonly grown in Ontario but could be grown in various regions based on zone, soil type and time allowance. They are not necessarily unknown, only deserving of more recognition and a place in Ontario gardens. So experiment, have fun, take a risk—you may just find that you wish you'd been growing some of them all along.

Finally, the pests and diseases section of the introduction deals with issues that afflict your garden plants from time to time.

Artichokes
Globe Artichokes

Cynara

Artichokes are one of those vegetables that require a little extra effort to grow successfully in parts of Ontario, and Canada for that matter, but they're well worth it if you're keen to follow a few simple rules. These members of the thistle family are tender perennials native to the Mediterranean. With a thick mulch, they may survive winter in southern Ontario. For the rest of the province, choose a quick-maturing cultivar and start very early to ensure success, and if all else fails, try again next year!

Starting

Start seeds indoors about 8 weeks before the last frost date, or up to 12 weeks before the last frost date if you have a very bright location or supplemental lighting available. Plant seeds into the largest size of peat pots. These plants don't like to have their roots disturbed, and you want to encourage them to grow as much as possible before they are planted into the garden. You can also purchase started plants, but you may have to shop early because

there is low availability, and often only specialty nurseries carry them.

Plant artichokes outdoors after the last frost date. These are very wide-spreading plants, so plant them at least 60 cm apart the first year and eventually up to 1.2 m apart if you overwinter them successfully.

Growing

Artichokes grow best in **full sun**, though they appreciate some after-noon shade in hotter locations. The soil should be **fertile, humus rich,**

moist and **well drained**. Mix compost into the soil in spring, and use a layer of compost on the soil as a mulch. These plants like plenty of water but don't like soggy soil. Replenish the compost mulch in mid-summer, if needed. If the buds are just beginning to form and heavy frost is expected, you can cover the plants with cotton sheets at night to extend the growing season.

As an alternative, mulch initially with straw rather than compost. Shredded leaves or hay can also be used to preserve the moisture in the soil and to control weeds while keeping the soil cool. Excessively warm soil may force the plants into a summer dormancy;

it's not likely that this will happen here, but it's better to be safe than sorry. Over time, add more mulch until you've reached a depth of 20 cm.

In southern Ontario, artichokes may survive winter. Plant them in a place where the soil stays warmest in winter, for example near a house foundation or other place where the soil doesn't freeze completely. This spot is often dry in summer, so mulch well to retain soil moisture. A layer of mulch 30–45 cm deep will help keep soil temperatures more consistent.

In late fall, cut the plants down to about 15 cm above soil level to prepare for winter. Cover the exposed stems with straw, hay or leaves to roughly 60 cm or more in depth. Ensure that there is adequate moisture in the ground surrounding the roots, without it being wet. Cover the mulch with a plastic sheet and anchor with rocks or pegs to protect the roots from excessive moisture. Once the danger of frost has passed in spring, uncover the mulched stems and feed with a dilute organic, natural fertilizer, such as fish fertilizer or compost tea. Feed again in 4 weeks, and again in fall.

In other parts of the province, you can either treat these plants like annuals or dig up the roots once the leaves die back in fall, clean off any soil and store them in slightly moistened peat or sphagnum moss in a cold, frost-free location for winter. Check them over winter, and if they are beginning to sprout, pot them and keep them in the brightest indoor location you can find until they can be planted outdoors again.

Harvesting

Artichokes produce one large flower bud on the central stalk and many smaller flower buds on the side shoots. The flower buds are rounded and made up of tightly packed scales. They are usually ready for harvest when they're about the size of a large lemon and the scales are still closed. Cut them about 2.5 cm below the head to encourage additional production of heads.

With luck and an early enough start, you should have a good crop the first year in fall. If overwintered successfully, artichokes generally flower earlier in the season, in June or July.

Tips

Artichoke plants make dramatic additions to vegetable and ornamental gardens. The flowers are quite stunning and can be used in fresh flower arrangements if not eaten while in bud form.

Recommended

C. scolymus forms a large clump of deeply lobed, pointy-tipped, grey-green leaves. It grows 60 cm–2 m tall and spreads 60 cm–1.2 m. In fall or sometimes summer, it bears large, scaled flower buds that open if not picked for eating. **'Green Globe'** is one of the most popular cultivars because it is tasty and is one of the quickest to mature and flower. **'Green Globe Improved'** does well in shorter seasons, has fewer spines and bears heavier fruit; however, it still needs to be started indoors in February, needing 180–240 days to mature. **'Imperial Star'** is one of the easiest to grow from seed, being specifically bred for annual production, and is ideal for colder climates or shorter seasons. It will bear fruit in the first season from seed, producing 6–8 mature buds, roughly 7–10 cm in diameter. **'Purple of Romagna'** is an Italian heirloom known for its tenderness and colour. **'Tempo'** is mature at 100 days, purple in colour and can be grown very successfully as an annual. **'Violetto'** is an Italian artichoke that produces purple heads. This variety takes longer to mature but is definitely worth experimenting with; start it roughly 10 weeks early indoors, if not earlier.

Problems and Pests

Rare problems with mould, root rot, slugs and aphids are possible.

Store unwashed artichokes in a sealed plastic bag in the refrigerator. Mist or sprinkle them with a bit of water to prevent dehydration. They will keep for up to 2 weeks.

'Green Globe' (above)

Arugula
Roquette, Salad Rocket
Diplotaxis, Eruca

Some people consider this peppery annual to be a vegetable, others a herb, and they're all right. Arugula is native to parts of Asia and southern Europe but has naturalized in parts of North America. It is relatively well-known and has experienced waves of popularity over the years. After close to two centuries of being overlooked, arugula is experiencing a new life in Canada. In fact, it's become quite fashionable, trendy even. I'd like to see it used in everyday cooking more often by the general public, rather than only in fancy-schmancy bistros and restaurants, because it has so much to offer.

Starting

Sow seed thinly, 0.5 cm deep and 45–60 cm apart, once the risk of frost has passed. Seed crops in succession, once or twice per week throughout the growing season. Crops in succession will provide you with young, tender leaves from spring to fall. Plant only what you can harvest. The seed germinates quickly, sprouting in just 3 days. Arugula is known to self-seed prolifically, so you may only have to seed it the one season.

Growing

Arugula prefers to grow in **full sun** or **partial shade. Cool, moist, rich** soil will help to produce more tender and less pungent leaves than those in dry, hot soil. Pinch the new leaves out frequently for use, and maintain a good level of moisture without keeping the soil too wet. Excessive fertilizer results in lush leaves lacking in flavour. Arugula can withstand light frosts.

Arugula is best grown either in a vegetable or herb garden setting, in the ground, outdoors; however, it is possible to grow it in pots. Make sure to sow the seed early in spring and use a bark, compost potting mix.

Harvesting

The leaves are aromatic, producing a peppery scent as they are harvested. They are best when picked tender, before the flower stems emerge. They become more pungent and somewhat bitter over time. The leaves are ready for harvest 6–8 weeks after sowing and should always be used fresh, as drying the leaves just diminishes the flavour. They do not freeze well either.

The flowers, seeds and an oil extract are also edible. The flowers, which taste a little on the citrus side, can be used as an edible garnish.

Tips

The leaves, though attractive, don't have much to offer in aesthetics. Arugula combines well with other herbs, including parsley, lovage, cilantro, basil, cress, dill, borage and salad burnet.

Recommended

D. tenuifolia (wild arugula) has a sharper flavour compared to the cultivated selections and is a favourite among chefs and cooks. It grows 30–40 cm tall. **'Discovery'** is a uniform, vigorous cultivar with an upright habit. It produces pungent leaves with a hint of sweetness in roughly 50 days from seed. **'Sylvetta'** is a perennial that grows into very dense, small bushes loaded with deeply lobed leaves. The flowers produced are also delicious.

You may come across a wild arugula that is completely different from the one recommended here. *D. muralis* is a perennial, producing more ornate leaves that are equally as pungent as those of *D. tenuifolia*. Turkish arugula (*Bunias orientalis*) produces leaves that resemble those of a dandelion. The flavour of the leaves of both plants diminishes almost entirely once the flowers appear. They also become more peppery in flavour as they age, but only before flower production.

E. vesicaria **subsp.** ***sativa*** (salad arugula, salad rocket, roquette) is an upright annual with toothed leaves on tall stems tipped with 4-petalled, white flowers with purple veins, reminiscent of scented geranium flowers. This grouping of arugula is considered to be the cultivated selections, as opposed to the wild selections. Slender, erect seedpods follow the flowers. It grows 60–90 cm tall but only 15–20 cm wide. **'Astro'** is ready for harvest in 38 days, producing a more mild flavour and rounded leaves. **'Runway'** is a vigorous grower, producing large, deeply lobed leaves. Harvest at 21 days for baby arugula. **'Surrey'** is mature in 21 days for baby leaves, 40 days for full-sized leaves. This late-bolting cultivar is rich and spicy.

Problems and Pests

Flea beetles, cutworms, aphids and thrips can all prey on arugula, but rarely, and they're all easily treatable with a sharp spray of water or an organic insecticidal soap. If you are concerned about possible pest problems, you can cover the emerging plants with a floating row cover.

Arugula is popular in Mediterranean cuisine, as well as in herbal butters, dressings and pesto, with or without basil.

Asparagus

Asparagus

The large, ferny growth that asparagus develops comes as quite a surprise to first-time growers who may only have seen tidy bunches of spears at the grocery store. Asparagus is a member of the lily family, and well-established plants can last a lifetime, producing tasty spears every spring.

Asparagus is dioecious—male and female flowers are borne on separate plants. Male plants are reputed to produce the greatest number of spears.

'Mary Washington'

Starting

Asparagus can be grown from seed, but it takes an average of 3 years until you get a full crop. Most people begin with 1-year-old crowns, or roots, purchased from the garden centre. A plant started from roots will be ready to begin harvesting the second spring.

Plant purchased roots into a well-prepared area. Work plenty of compost into the bed, then dig a trench or hole about 45 cm deep. Lay the roots 45–60 cm apart from each other or other plants. Cover the roots with 5–10 cm of soil and, as they sprout up, gradually cover them with more soil until the trench or hole is filled. Water and mulch well.

Plant seeds indoors in flats or peat pots about 6–8 weeks before you will be planting them into the garden. Transfer seedlings to larger pots if they get too big before the last frost date has passed and you can move them outside. The first year, plant the

First-year plant (left); young spears emerging (right)

seedlings at the soil level they are at in their pots. Keep them well watered and mulch them with compost. The second season, the rooted seedlings can be planted, as described earlier, as roots or crowns in a trench. The third season they should be mature enough to produce a full crop of spears.

Growing

Asparagus grows well in **full sun** or **partial shade** with protection from the hot afternoon sun. The soil should be **fertile, humus rich, moist** and **well drained**. Apply a 10 cm layer of compost in spring and late summer. Weed regularly; this plant is most productive if it doesn't have a lot of competition from other plants.

Harvesting

As mentioned, asparagus spears that were started from roots are ready to be harvested 2 years after planting; spears started from seeds are ready in 3 years. Snap or cut the spears off at ground level for up to about 4 weeks in spring and early summer. When new spears are thinner than a pencil, you should stop harvesting and let the plants grow in. Add a new layer of compost to the soil when you have finished harvesting.

Tips

This hardy perennial plant is a welcome treat in spring and a beautiful addition to the back of a border.

Recommended

A. officinalis forms an airy mound of ferny growth. It grows 60 cm–1.5 m tall and spreads 60 cm–1.2 m. Small, white, summer flowers are followed by bright red berries, which can be collected for starting new plants. **'Jersey Giant'** is known for its high yield and production of the largest spears, while **'Jersey Knight'** produces premium quality spears up to 2 cm thick. **'Jersey Supreme'** is known for its sheer abundance of spears produced once established, up to 4.5 kg per season. **'Martha Washington'** and **'Mary Washington'** are traditional, productive strains, while **'Guelph Millennium'** was developed by the University of Guelph after 19 years of research and is known for its consistently high yields. **'Purple Passion'** produces sweet and tender spears, more so than green varieties. There is a slightly lesser yield with this cultivar because it is not often predominantly male. The purple spears turn green when cooked. **'Viking'** is one of the hardiest varieties available.

Problems and Pests

Rust can be a problem, so choose resistant cultivars.

Asparagus has been a cultivated vegetable crop for over 2000 years.

Beans

Phaseolus, Vicia

This incredibly diverse group of legumes is sure to please everyone; there are few things as delicious as fresh beans for dinner, straight out of the garden. Most people are familiar with the string bean, but there is so much more to this group of vegetables. The selection is almost endless.

Starting

Beans are quite possibly one of the easiest plants to grow from seed. The seeds are large and easy to handle, and they sprout quickly in warm, moist soil. Plant them directly in the garden after the last frost date has passed and the soil has warmed up. They can be planted 10–20 cm apart.

Growing

Beans grow best in **full sun**, but they tolerate some light afternoon shade. The soil should be of **average fertility** and **well drained**. Bush beans are self-supporting, but climbing beans need a pole or trellis to grow up. The support structure should be in place at planting time to avoid disturbing the young plants or damaging their roots.

Bush beans can become less productive and look unattractive as summer wears on. Pull them up and plant something else in their place, or plant them with companions that mature more slowly to fill in the space left by the faded bean plants.

Harvesting

The most important thing to remember when harvesting beans is to do so only when the foliage is dry. Touching wet foliage encourages the spread of disease.

Different types of beans should be picked at different stages in their development. Green, runner, wax or snap beans are picked once the pod is a good size but still young and

Runner beans growing on a trellis (below)

tender. As they mature, they become stringy, woody and dry. Beans that are eaten as immature seeds should be picked when the pods are full and the seeds are fleshy and moist.

Beans for drying are left to mature on the plant. Once the plant begins to die back and before the seedpods open, cut the entire plant off at ground level, leaving the nitrogen-fixing roots to enrich the soil, and hang it upside down indoors to finish drying. You can then remove the beans from the pods and store them in airtight containers in a cool, dry place. The beans will keep for 10–12 months.

Tips

Beans are very ornamental, with attractive leaves and plentiful flowers. Climbing beans can be grown up fences, trellises, obelisks and poles to create a screen or feature planting. Bush beans can be used to make low, temporary hedges or can be planted in small groups in a border.

Recommended

P. coccineus (runner bean) is a vigorous climbing plant with red or sometimes white or bicoloured flowers. **'Scarlet Runner'** has bright red flowers and is one of the best and best-known cultivars. The beans can be eaten with the pod when they are young and tender, or the plants can be left to mature and the pink and purple spotted beans can be dried. Plants produce edible beans in 70 days but need about 100 days for dry beans. **'Scarlet Empire'** is ready for harvest in 85 days, producing longer, smoother, stringless pods. **'Pantheon'** is another stringless selection. It is ready in 75 days and has flat, juicy pods 2.5 cm wide and 25 cm long. **'St. George'** is an award-winning selection that has smooth, fleshy pods 30 cm long. This early bean has good snap with little fibre when picked regularly.

P. lunatus (lima bean) may be climbing or bush, depending on the cultivar. The beans are eaten as immature seeds and should be picked when the pods are plump but the seeds are still tender. They take 70–85 days to mature. **'Fordhook'** is a popular bush variety, and **'King**

of the Garden' is a good climbing selection.

P. vulgaris (wax bean, green bean, bush bean, pole bean, snap bean, dry bean) is probably the largest group of beans and includes bush beans and pole beans. Some are eaten immature in the pod, and others are grown to maturity and used as dry beans. Bush bean cultivars may be yellow, such as **'Gold Rush'** and **'Sunburst'**; green, such as **'Ambra'** and **'Stallion'**; or purple-podded, such as **'Royal Burgundy.'** Purple beans turn bright green when cooked. Bush beans take 50–60 days to mature.

Other noteworthy bush bean selections include the following. **'Golden Teepee'** is a golden yellow bean that grows 16 cm long on a very compact plant that grows 40–45 cm tall. Maturing in 48 days, the flavour produced by this bean is second to none. **'Purple Teepee'** is similar in size and flavour but purple in colour. **'Concador,'** a dwarf bush bean, is ideal for containers, producing 12 cm long, slender, pale yellow beans for a longer period than most other selections. **'Nash Green'** has been adapted to warm Ontario summers. It has an excellent yield and heat tolerance. **'Tema'** is ready in 52 days and tolerates cool, wet soils. It produces for a longer period than most and holds its flavour. **'Rocdor'** is ready in 53 days and has a natural buttery flavour. This French gourmet bush bean is great for freezing and is a heavy yielder.

Pole beans, such as **'Blue Lake'** and **'Kentucky Blue,'** take 50–55 days to mature. **'Bush Blue Lake'** is a dwarf bush selection with dark bluish, 15–16 cm long beans that are good for canning, freezing or eating fresh.

Dry beans are usually bush plants and take about 100 days to mature.

They include kidney, pinto and navy beans. A popular selection for home growers is the red and white spotted **'Jacob's Cattle.'** **'Red Noodle'** produces beans that are red-burgundy in colour and reach lengths of 40–50 cm. They're produced in clusters and are sweet in taste. The colour fades when cooked, but they're good enough to eat fresh.

Shell beans (wren's eggs, horticultural beans, bird eggs, speckled cranberries, October beans) come in both pole and dwarf varieties and can produce big harvests in small gardens. Most beans can be used as shell (or shelling) beans, which have the pods removed before they are cooked or dried. One selection that is highly coveted for shell bean use is **'Supremo,'** which is ready for harvest in 85 days.

V. faba (broad bean, fava bean) **'Sweet Lorane'** has great flavour and cold hardiness. It is ready for harvest in 90–140 days. It produces fragrant flowers followed by tough-skinned pods. They must be soaked overnight before using. **'Windsor'** grows 90 cm–1.2 m tall and produces pods 12–20 cm long, containing 5–7 beans. These wonderfully thick broad beans are mature in 4–5 months and shell very easily. **'Crimson Flowered'** is mature in 95 days and produces crimson flowers and upright, tasty pods. This selection is ideal for growing in containers, borders or as an ornamental vegetable.

Problems and Pests

Pick beans only when plants are dry to reduce the spread of disease. Problems with leaf spot, bacterial blight, rust, bean beetles and aphids can occur. Disease-infected plants should be destroyed, not composted, once you've harvested what you can.

Climbing beans are popular among gardeners with limited space because you can get more beans for less space.

Legumes (including beans) are known for being able to fix nitrogen from the air into the soil through a symbiotic relationship with bacteria, which attach to the roots as small nodules. The bacteria turn the nitrogen from the air into useable nitrogen for the plant; in return, the plant feeds and supports the bacteria. The bacteria are present in most soils and are also available for purchase as a soil inoculant. Some bean seeds are also pre-treated with the bacteria.

Beets

Beta

Beets are not only delicious but also versatile. The plump, rounded or cylindrical roots are the most commonly eaten part. The tops are also edible, are incredibly nutritious and can be compared in flavour to spinach and Swiss chard. Beets and Swiss chard are closely related, both being members of the genus *Beta*.

Starting

The corky, wrinkled seed of a beet is actually a dry fruit that contains several tiny seeds. Plant it directly in the garden around the last frost date. Even if you space the seeds 7–15 cm apart, you will probably have to thin a bit because several plants can sprout from each fruit. Beets are fairly quick to mature, and a second crop can often be planted in mid-summer for a fall harvest.

Growing

Beets grow well in **full sun** or **partial shade**. They grow best in cool weather. The soil should be **fertile, moist** and **well drained**. Mulch lightly with compost to maintain moisture and improve soil texture.

Harvesting

Beets mature in 45–80 days, depending on the variety. Short-season beets are best for immediate eating and preserving, and long-season beets are the better choice for storing over winter. Pick beets as soon as they are big enough to eat. They are tender when young but can become woody as they mature.

You can pick beet leaves without pulling up the entire beet if you want to use them for fresh or steamed greens. Don't pull all the leaves off a beet; just remove a few at a time from any one plant.

Tips

Beets have attractive red-veined, dark green foliage. These plants look good when planted in small groups in a border, and they make interesting edging plants. They can even be included in large mixed container plantings.

*Just a few for pickled beets.

Recommended

B. vulgaris forms a dense rosette of glossy, dark green leaves, often with deep red stems and veins. It grows 20–45 cm tall and spreads 10–20 cm. There are many cultivars available, but the following are some of the more common selections. **'Alto'** produces a very sweet, natural flavour and uniform roots. The smooth, red skin and flesh is free from rings and blemishes and often stands slightly above ground but can be covered or mounded with soil. **'Bull's Blood'** matures in 45 days as a salad leaf, and 70 days for roots. Its dark, rich foliage is commonly used as a salad green. **'Detroit Dark Red'** has dark red beets and was developed from the heirloom **'Detroit.'** **'Golden Detroit'** has red skin and yellow flesh.

'Early Wonder' and **'Red Ace'** are good red, round cultivars. **'Pablo'** is a bright red baby beet. **'Wodan'** is a bright red hybrid with a rounded shape, sweet, earthy flavour and young leaves that can be used as an alternative to spinach. This hybrid is ideal for pickling, particularly as a baby beet. **'Ruby Queen'** is an early selection, ready in 48–55 days. This smooth-skinned, buttery sweet beet is bright red with short tops. **'Cylindra Formanova'** produces carrot-like roots 15 cm long and is ideal for slicing or freezing.

Novelty beet selections have been quite popular lately because of their colouration, and often shape, including the following. **'Albina Vereduna'** is ready for harvest in

70 days, producing crisp, white flesh with a sweet flavour surpassing most red selections. The curly and wavy leaves are beautiful and also delicious and nutritious in salads. **'Chioggia'** is an heirloom cultivar that produces red-and-white-ringed roots. **'Dolce Di Chioggia'** is ready in 55 days, producing red-and-white-striped flesh with a sweet flavour. When cut, the concentric circles of colour from this heirloom variety can be used raw or cooked, as can the leaves. **'Rodina'** has a red, cylindrical root. **'Touchstone Gold'** is ready for harvest is 60 days, producing bright green foliage and sweet, tender, golden roots with blushed skins and yellow flesh. This selection is one of the best for pickling.

Problems and Pests

Beets are generally problem free, but occasional trouble with scab, root maggots and flea beetles can occur.

Never fear if you get beet juice on your clothing; it won't stain. Dyers have been unsuccessfully trying to find a fixative for beet juice for centuries. Chemists inform us that the red molecule in beets is very large and doesn't adhere to other molecules, so a fixative is unlikely to ever be found.

Broccoli

Brassica

Although usually thought of as a vegetable, broccoli could more accurately be called an edible flower. It is the large, dense flower clusters that are generally eaten, though the stems and leaves are also edible, not to mention jam-packed with minerals, vitamins and micronutrients.

Starting

Broccoli can be started from seed indoors or planted directly into the garden. Sow seeds indoors 4–6 weeks before the last frost date, and plant seedlings out or direct sow into the garden around the last frost date, usually 30 cm apart.

Growing

Broccoli grows best in **full sun**. The soil should be **fertile, moist** and **well drained**. Broccoli performs best in cooler weather. Mix compost into the soil, and add a layer of mulch to keep the soil moist. Don't let this plant dry out excessively or it will delay flowering.

Harvesting

Broccoli forms a central head (broccoli), and some varieties also produce side shoots. Pick the heads by cutting them cleanly from the plant with a sharp knife. If you leave them for too long on the plant, the bright yellow flowers will open.

Choosing a side-shoot-producing plant versus a main-head-only variety is a matter of personal preference. If you have a large family or plan to freeze some florets, you may prefer a large-headed selection. If there are only a few people in the household, or you want to enjoy the broccoli for longer without storing any, you may prefer the small-headed varieties that produce plenty of side shoots.

Tips

Broccoli, with its blue-green foliage, is an interesting accent plant. Tuck small groups of it into your borders and mixed beds for a striking contrast.

This plant is susceptible to quite a few pest and disease problems, and spacing it out in small groups rather than planting it in rows helps reduce the severity of the potential problems.

Recommended

B. oleracea **var.** *botrytis* is an upright plant with a stout, leafy central stem. Flowers form at the top of the plant and sometimes on side shoots that emerge from just above each leaf. Plants grow 30–90 cm tall and spread 30–45 cm. Maturity dates vary from 45 to 100 days. '**Belstar**' produces well-domed, small-beaded, deep green heads. '**Martha**' is an early variety, short and compact in habit and very heat tolerant. It bears large heads with a greyish blue cast and small beads. '**Calbrese**' ('Calabria') produces plenty of side shoots. '**De Cicco**' has edible leaves and produces many side shoots. '**Gypsy**' produces a large central head and is one of the most heat-tolerant

'Broccolo Verde Romanesco'

cultivars. **'Nutri-Bud'** is an early-maturing cultivar that produces plenty of side shoots after the main head is cut. **'Packman'** is an earlier selection, ready in 55 days. It bears large, domed heads with medium-sized beads. It is also one of the most prolific side shoot producers. It is very tolerant of hot weather and can be planted in succession. **'Premium Crop'** is an All America Selections winner that is early to mature and produces plenty of side shoots.

Broccoli is also available in novelty selections. **'Broccoli Mini Hybrid Apollo'** (asparagus broccoli) is ready in 50 days for the mini form, or before total maturity, which averages 100 days. This selection has the appearance of headless broccoli. The main floret is harvested first, followed by the abundant side shoots that are tender, sweet and delicious. **'Broccolo Verde Romanesco'** is sometimes known as broccoflower because of its appearance, resembling a cross between cauliflower and broccoli. Its texture is similar to both, but it tastes more like broccoli. **'Love Me Tender'** is a sweet, mild selection with tender stalks and large, green heads that are ready in roughly 62 days. It sometimes produces heads with a blush of purple and reddish yellow. **'Summer Purple'** is ready for harvest in 100 days and is ideal for warmer parts of the province. It produces tasty loose, purple clusters in large quantities.

B. rapa ruvo (raab, broccoletto) is a delicious, quick-sprouting form of broccoli. **'Cima de Rapa'** is a selection that produces spicy, edible leaves, shoots and flower buds—what some might call mini broccoli. **'Spring Raab'** is ready in 42 days, producing large plants that are very slow to bolt. This selection is considered to be one of the more versatile ones for growing throughout the season with successive plantings for continuous harvests.

Problems and Pests

Problems with cutworms, leaf miners, caterpillars, root maggots, cabbage white butterflies, white rust, downy mildew and powdery mildew can occur. Avoid planting any Brassica in the same spot in successive years.

Until about 60 years ago, broccoli was not known as an individual, but as a type of cauliflower, its cousin.

Cabbage white butterflies are common pests for all members of the Brassica family, and their tiny green caterpillar larvae can be tough to spot in a head of broccoli. Break heads into pieces and soak them in salted water for 10 or so minutes before cooking. Doing so kills the larvae and causes them to float to the surface.

Brussels Sprouts

Brassica

Love them or hate them, Brussels sprouts are at the very least
a garden curiosity. The sprouts form on the stout central stem at
the base of each leaf. By fall, the display is unique and eye-catching.

Starting

Brussels sprouts can be purchased as small transplants in spring, or seeds can be started indoors about 6 weeks before you expect to transplant the seedlings into the garden. Sowing the seeds into peat pots or pellets makes trasplanting easy. Space the seedlings 45–60 cm apart, depending on the variety; check the seed packet or plant tag.

Growing

Brussels sprouts grow well in **full sun**. The soil should be **fertile, moist** and **well drained**. Brussels sprouts need a fairly long growing season to produce sprouts of any appreciable size, so they should be planted out as early as possible. Regular moisture encourages them to mature quickly, so keep the soil well mulched. Once you see sprouts starting to form, you may wish to remove some of the stem leaves to give the sprouts more room to grow.

Harvesting

Pick sprouts as soon as they are large and plump, but before they begin to open. A light frost can improve the flavour of the sprouts. The entire plant can be pulled up, and if you remove the roots, leaves and top of the plant, the sprouts can be stored on the stem in a cool place for up to 4 weeks. Be sure to keep an eye on them because they can go bad quickly. They can also be frozen for later use.

Tips

Brussels sprouts create a leafy backdrop for your flowering annuals and perennials all summer; then, just as the garden is fading, they create an interesting focal point as the plump little sprouts develop.

Recommended

B. oleracea var. *gemnifera* is an upright plant that develops a single leafy stem. Sprouts form at the base of each leaf along the stem. The leaves are blue-green, often with white midribs and stems. '**Bitesize**' is a sweet selection that produces well-spaced heads that are easy to harvest. The heads remain firm on the stem for a long period of time compared to other varieties. '**Catskill**' produces heads, or sprouts, with a cabbage flavour, and in great abundance. They're very tender and small, reaching only 2–5 cm across, on very strong stalks. '**Trafalgar**' produces a heavy crop of super sweet, medium-sized sprouts that keep for a long period on the stalk. '**Bedford Fillbasket**,' '**Jade Cross**' and '**Vancouver**' are popular cultivars. '**Fallstaff**' is a late variety, maturing in 200 days, and is best started indoors long before last frost. It is well-suited to southern regions of the province. It bears purple-red heads with a milder and nuttier flavour than green selections. The colour intensifies after a frost and is retained when cooked.

Problems and Pests

Problems with cutworms, leaf miners, caterpillars, root maggots, aphids, cabbage white butterfly larvae, white rust, downy mildew and powdery mildew can occur.

To avoid overcooking Brussels sprouts, cut an X about one-quarter of the way through each sprout to help the inside cook at the same rate as the outside.

Cabbage & Oriental Cabbage

Brassica

Cabbages of every size, shape and texture are easy to grow, and they create a dense, leafy, often colourful display. They come in three forms: green with smooth leaves, green with very crinkled leaves and red or purple, usually with smooth leaves.

Starting

Start seeds indoors about 4–6 weeks before you plan to transplant the seedlings outdoors. You can also direct sow cabbage into the garden around the last frost date as long as the soil has warmed up a bit. Early selections can be planted up to 30 cm apart, while late selections can be planted up to 45 cm apart. If you find average cabbages too large, plant them closer together to get smaller, tighter heads.

Growing

Cabbages grow best in **full sun**. They prefer cool growing conditions and benefit from mulch to retain moisture during hot weather. The soil should be **fertile, moist** and **well drained**.

Oriental cabbage likes the same conditions but is more tolerant of warm, humid weather than some of the other members of the Brassica family, making it a useful addition to hotter Canadian gardens.

Harvesting

The leaves of young cabbage plants can be eaten. When a good-sized head has developed, cut it cleanly from the plant. Smaller heads often develop once the main head has been cut.

Oriental cabbage comes in two basic forms: solid heads that are cut whole, and looser heads with leaves that can be removed as needed.

Cabbages are frost hardy, and the last of them can be left in the ground through fall, then stored in a cold,

'Early Jersey Wakefield'

Savoy cabbages (above and below)

frost-free location. Cabbages that take a long time to mature generally store better than quick-maturing types.

Tips

Grow several varieties of cabbages because the different colours, textures and maturing times create a more interesting display, whether in rows or mixed into your borders.

Oriental cabbage can be grown in containers, where it can be combined with other edible or flowering plants. Dotted through a border, it creates a low but upright feature, adding its unique colour and form.

Recommended

B. oleracea var. *capitata* (cabbage) is a low, leafy rosette that develops a dense head over summer. Leaves may be green, blue-green, red or purple and smooth or crinkled. It matures in 60–140 days, depending on the variety.

Some popular smooth-leaved, green varieties are **'January King,' 'Bartolo,' 'Early Jersey Wakefield,' 'Lennox'** and **'Parel.' 'Blue Vantage'** is a mid-season selection, producing large, dense, short-cored, blue-green heads. It is best eaten fresh. **'Danish Ball-head'** is a late variety with light green heads 18–20 cm in diameter. This selection matures in 110 days.

'Early Copenhagen Market' is ready for harvest in 66 days. The light greenish blue heads weigh 1–1.5 kg. **'Show-off'** lives up to its name, with light green, 5.5–7 kg heads with great flavour. **'Caraflex'** is one of the more interesting selections because it is pointed like a teardrop. It is incredibly sweet and is one of the most tender cabbages to grow in Canada. Popular in Europe, this pointed cabbage can be used just like any other cabbage. It's ready 50 days after transplanting.

A smooth-leaved green variety

Popular red cabbages include **'Buscaro,' 'Red Acre Early,' 'Red Drumhead,' 'Red Express'** and **'Ruby Dynasty.' 'Super Red 80'** is an early hybrid with medium-sized, deep purple-red heads and a superior peppery flavour.

B. rapa* subsp. *chinensis (pac choi, bok choi) forms a loose clump of blue-green leaves with thick, fleshy, white or light green stems. There are three types: green stem, white stem and specialty. **'Hanakan'** is a compact Japanese green stem hybrid that is ready to harvest in 45 days. **'Dwarf Pak Choi'** (baby bok choi) is a white-stemmed variety. It is mild in flavour, with white stems and ribs and deep green leaves. Harvest when it is 10 cm tall. **'Golden Yellow'** is a specialty hybrid that bears yellowish green leaves from root to tip. The texture is softer than other varieties but the flavour is the same. **'Red Violet Tatsoi'** is a deep purple variety.

B. rapa* subsp. *pekinensis (Chinese cabbage, nappa cabbage) forms

Popular crinkled or savoy types include **'Savoy Blue,' 'Savoy King,' 'Taler'** and **'Wirosa.' 'Melissa'** produces dark green heads and deeper savoyed leaves than other mid-season varieties.

a dense head of tightly packed leaves. There are four types: barrel head, loose head, fluffy top and Michihili. **'Optiko'** has a barrel shape and prominent white veins and ribs. It can be used like a savoy cabbage. It matures faster than most others and is mild tasting with a crisp texture. **'Vitaminna,'** a loose head type, is common in Japanese homes because of its dark green leaves, white stems, slowness to bolt and high concentration of vitamin A. **'Kaisin Hakusai'** is a fluffy top cabbage with frilly outer leaves that become more blanched toward the centre. **'Green Rocket,'** a Michihili type, resembles an endive or chicory head, but in jumbo size. This Chinese cabbage is grown for its sweetness.

The tight heads are more mild and tender than western cabbages.

Problems and Pests

Problems with cutworms, leaf miners, caterpillars, root maggots, aphids, cabbage white butterfly larvae, white rust, downy mildew and powdery mildew can occur.

All members of the Brassica family are susceptible to many of the same pests and diseases. Don't plant them in the same spot 2 years in a row, particularly if you've had disease problems in that area.

An interesting addition to the garden, Oriental cabbage is also a tasty ingredient in stir-fries and soups.

A mix of Oriental cabbage varieties and bok choi

Carrots

Daucus

For many years, decades in fact, there were no more than two or three types of carrot to grow in any given place in Canada; today there is an endless array of hybrids, cultivars and heirloom varieties to choose from. You could choose two different types each growing season for the rest of your life and never get close to growing all of them…so experiment and try something new!

Starting

Carrots can be sown directly into the garden once the last frost date has passed and the soil has warmed up. The seeds are very tiny and can be difficult to plant evenly. Mix the tiny seeds with sand before you sow them to spread them more evenly and reduce the need for thinning. You can also purchase seeds that have been coated with clay to make them easier to handle. Cover the seeds only very lightly with sand or compost because they can't sprout through too much soil. Keep the seedbed moist to encourage even germination.

Growing

Carrots grow best in **full sun**. The soil should be **average to fertile, well drained** and **deeply prepared**. Because you are growing carrots for the root, you need to be sure that the soil is loose and free of rocks to a depth of 20–30 cm. This gives carrots plenty of space to develop and makes them easier to pull up when they are ready for eating. If your soil is very rocky or shallow, you may wish to plant carrots in raised beds to provide deeper, looser soil; or just grow shorter varieties of carrots.

Spacing carrots is a gradual process. As the carrots develop, pull a few of the more crowded ones out, leaving room for the others to fill in. This thinning process will give you an indication of how well they are developing and when they will be ready to harvest. The root can be eaten at all stages of development.

Harvesting

Never judge carrots by their greens. Big, bushy tops are no indication that carrots are ready for picking. As the roots develop, you will often see the top of the carrots at or just above soil level—a better indication of their development. You can pull carrots up by getting a good grip on the greens in loose enough soil, but you may need a garden fork to dig them up in a heavier soil.

To keep carrots for a long time, store them in a cold, frost-free place in containers of moistened sand.

Tips

Carrots make an excellent ornamental grouping or edging plant. The feathery foliage provides an attractive background for flowers and plants with ornamental foliage. Carrots can also be grown in containers with adequate depth for root growth.

Recommended

D. carota* var. *sativus forms a bushy mound of feathery foliage. It matures in 50–75 days. The edible roots may be orange, red, yellow, white or purple. They come in a variety of shapes, from long and slender to short and round. The type you choose will depend on the flavour you like, how

'Cosmic Purple' (above)

long you need to store them and how suitable your soil is.

Some of the more standard selections include the following. **'Little Finger'** produces baby carrots. **'Napoli'** is an early-maturing, sweet carrot. **'Mignon'** is ready for harvest in 70 days, producing rich, tender, orange roots that were bred for growing as baby carrots. Because of this trait, 'Mignon' is ideal for successive sowings throughout the growing season. **'Bolero'** is a carrot for the most difficult climates, producing high yields, strong tops and huge roots, with a superior level of disease resistance. **'Danvers'** produces 20 cm long roots with firm flesh, an excellent sweet flavour and strong tops, which makes for easy pulling. **'Fly Away'** was bred to be unattractive to flies, very sweet and

adaptable to tough environmental conditions. **'Resistafly'** is rust fly resistant. **'Royal Chantenay'** is an heirloom carrot with a deep orange core. **'Scarlet Nantes'** ('Nantes'), one of the most popular carrots, is a sweet heirloom carrot. **'Sweetness'** is an extra-early Nantes carrot, ready in 55 days bearing heavy yields of 15–20 cm long carrots. **'Mini Sweet'** is ready for harvest in 60 days and is very small and slim, averaging 10 cm in length, orange-red in colour and very tender in texture. This carrot is great raw, straight out of the soil.

There are also many novelty selections, based on colour, shape and so on. **'Atomic Red'** is a tapered, bright red carrot, measuring up to 30 cm long and 3–5 cm in diameter. This crispy carrot has a great taste regardless of its size and intensifies in colour when cooked. **'Cosmic Purple'** has smooth, purple skin and coreless, orange flesh. The 18 cm long roots have a sweet flavour, but the colour fades after cooking, so enjoy this selection raw in a salad. **'Nutri Red'** is a purple-red carrot high in lycopene, a precursor to beta-carotene. **'Purple Haze'** is a dark (almost black) purple-skinned, orange-fleshed carrot. **'White Satin'** is a white Nantes carrot with exceptionally sweet flesh. It has an excellent yield, is ready in 72 days and can grow up to 23 cm long. **'Rainbow Mix'** is often found in seed catalogues, offering a variety of carrot selections in different colours, maturity periods, flavours and sizes, but all are in the pastel shades, including peach, orange, yellow, white and purple.

Problems and Pests

Carrot rust flies and root maggots can sometimes be troublesome.

Hill up the soil around the tops to keep them covered throughout the growing process.

'Mini Sweet' (above)

Cauliflower

Brassica

Maybe it's not everyone's favourite, but with the interesting assortment of colours now available, cauliflower can create quite an interesting display in the late-summer or fall garden, not to mention how tasty it can be. Tuck a few plants here and there in your mixed borders to shake things up a bit and to increase your harvest.

Starting

Cauliflower can be sown directly into the garden around the last frost date, or you can start it indoors about 4 weeks before you plan to set it outdoors. Standard-sized heads should be spaced 30–45 cm apart; smaller selections can be planted closer together.

Growing

Cauliflower grows best in **full sun**. The soil should be **fertile, moist** and **well drained**. This plant doesn't like persistently hot weather (more than 2 weeks with temperatures over 28° C), but it's rarely a problem, even in comparatively hot Ontario gardens. Cauliflower must have a rich soil that stays evenly moist, or heads may form poorly, if at all. Mix plenty of compost into the soil, and mulch with compost to help keep the soil moist.

Harvesting

Unlike broccoli, cauliflower does not develop secondary heads once the main one is cut. Cut the head cleanly from the plant when it is mature. You can then compost the plant.

Tips

White cauliflower may turn yellow or greenish unless some of the leaves are tied over the head to shade it from the sun. Tie some of the outer leaves together over the head with elastic or string when you first notice the head forming.

Unlike white cauliflower, the purple-, green-, yellow- or orange-headed varieties need no shading while they develop. The coloured selections are pretty when planted into mixed ornamental gardens.

Recommended

B. oleracea var. *botrytis* is leafy and upright with dense, edible flower clusters in the centre of the plant. Most selections take 70–85 days to mature, though some mature in as few as 45 days.

Popular white-headed cultivars include **'Early Dawn,' 'Snowball'** and **'Symphony.' 'Early Snowball'** takes 50 days from sowing to produce bright white heads with deep curds. This large selection is also great for freezing. **'Snow Crown'** is ready in 53 days and is considered to be one of the easiest selections to grow early in the season due to its vigour and tough constitution. It produces medium-sized, domed heads up to 20 cm across.

'Graffiti' and **'Violet Queen'** are purple-headed cultivars. 'Graffiti' is the later selection, bearing dark purple heads in 80 days. Unlike 'Violet Queen,' it produces more of a "true" cauliflower head, rather

than a cluster of tinier heads, on very large plants.

Green-headed cultivars include **'Green Harmony'** and **'Veronica,'** whose florets form pointed, tapering peaks. **'Romanesco White Gold'** has a space-age appearance, producing spirally, lime green florets with a broccoli flavour and cauliflower texture. **'Broccoverde'** is another green-headed cauliflower. It has medium-sized, domed heads. This selection is very sweet and tolerates warmer zones.

'Cheddar' is a popular orange-headed cultivar. **'Orange Bouquet'** is ready in 60 days, producing pale orange heads high in vitamin A.

Problems and Pests

Problems with cutworms, leaf miners, caterpillars, root maggots, aphids, cabbage white butterfly larvae, white rust, downy mildew and powdery mildew can occur.

Cauliflower was once touted as a difficult vegetable to grow, but opinions have changed dramatically over the years. It is now considered to be quite easy to grow and is highly regarded by most gardeners.

Celery & Celeriac

Apium

Tender, ribbed stalks of celery fresh from the garden are quite different than store-bought celery. The flavour of unblanched stems is
much stronger but much appreciated by many gardeners, and the
wide variety of uses for this veggie far surpasses the ever-faithful
CheezWhiz or peanut butter spread on top.

Celeriac (above)

Starting

Celery seed should be started indoors at least 8 weeks and up to 12 weeks before you plan to transplant it outdoors. Be patient; seed can take up to 3 weeks to germinate. Be sure to keep the planting medium moist, but not soggy. Plant out once the last frost date has passed and the soil has warmed up.

Growing

Celery and celeriac grow best in **full sun** but enjoy light or afternoon shade in hot weather. The soil should be **fertile, humus rich, moist** and **well drained**. Allowing the soil to dry out too much will give you a poor quality, bad-tasting vegetable. Mulch plants to conserve moisture.

In late summer, you can mound soil around the celery stalks, wrap them

in newspaper or surround the base of each plant with a milk carton with the top and bottom cut out to shade them from the sun, which will encourage the development of the pale green or blanched stems we are familiar with. Unblanched stalks have a stronger flavour that some people prefer. Celeriac needs no blanching.

Harvesting

Celery stalks can be harvested 1–2 at a time from each plant for most of summer. If you are blanching the stems before picking them, they will be ready for harvesting 2–3 weeks after the stalks are covered. A light touch of frost can sweeten the flavour of the celery.

Celeriac should be harvested before the first fall frost. Pull plants up, remove the leaves and store the knobby roots the same way you would beets or carrots, in a cold, frost-free location in a container of moistened sand.

Tips

Celery and celeriac have light green leaves that create a very bushy backdrop for flowering plants with less attractive, spindly growth.

Recommended

A. graveolens var. *dulce* (celery) is a bushy, upright plant with attractive, light to bright green foliage. It matures in 80–120 days. **'Celery XP 266,' 'Conquistador,' 'Golden Self-Blanching,' 'Red Stalk'** and **'Utah 52-70'** are popular cultivars. **'Victoria'** is an earlier variety, with strong stalks, high resistance to bolting and a crisp texture. **'Tango'** is ready in 80 days, producing stronger flavour than most. The stalks are tender, with less fibre, and the plant overall is more tolerant to excessive heat and moisture stress.

A. graveolens var. *secalinum* **'Affina'** (cutting celery) is grown more for the greens than anything else. The stalks don't develop like other cultivars do, so this selection is considered to be an immature form of celery. The plants are ready for harvest in 120 days, if not sooner, producing a clump of slender stems and bright green leaves for cutting. Harvest and use the leaves readily

to promote further, denser growth throughout the growing season.

A. graveolens var. *rapaceum* (celeriac) forms a bushy, bright green plant that develops a thick, knobby, bulbous root. It matures in 100–120 days or more. **'Diamant'** and **'Giant Prague'** are popular cultivars. **'Monarch'** is a late variety, ready in 160 days. It bears smooth, cream-coloured roots that are easy to wash clean, and it is easier to grow than your standard garden variety of celeriac. **'Rowena'** is an early selection, ready in roughly 105 days. It vigorously bears round heads and is slow to bolt. It's also a good keeper once harvested.

Problems and Pests

Problems with fungal blight, mosaic virus, fusarium yellows, bacterial and fungal rot, leaf spot and caterpillars can occur.

Chard
Swiss Chard
Beta

Chard is one of the most useful vegetables to include in your garden. The tasty leaves and stems can be harvested all summer, and the wide range of colours makes it a valuable ornamental addition to beds, borders and even container gardens.

Starting

The corky, wrinkled seed of chard is actually a dry fruit that contains several tiny seeds. Plant the dry fruit directly in the garden around the last frost date. You will probably have to thin the plants a bit even if you space the seeds 7–15 cm apart because several plants can sprout from each fruit.

Growing

Chard grows well in **full sun** or **partial shade**. It grows best in cool weather. The soil should be **fertile, moist** and **well drained**. Mulch lightly with compost to maintain moisture and improve soil texture.

Harvesting

Chard matures quickly, and a few leaves can be plucked from each plant every week or so all summer. You can generally start picking leaves about a month after the seed sprouts and continue to do so until the plant is killed back by frost.

Tips

Chard has very decorative foliage. Although the leaves are usually glossy green, the stems and veins are often brightly coloured in shades of red, pink, white, yellow or orange. When planted in small groups in your borders, chard adds a colourful touch. The bushy, clumping habit also makes it well suited to mixed container plantings.

Recommended

B. vulgaris* subsp. *cicla forms a
clump of glossy green, purple, red
or bronze leaves that are often
deeply crinkled or savoyed. Stems
and veins may be pale green, white,
yellow, orange, pink, red or purple.
Plants grow 20–45 cm tall and
spread about 30 cm. Popular cultivars include **'Bright Lights,'** an
All America Selections winner that
produces a mix of red, white, pink,
green, orange, gold, violet and yellow stems, mostly solid but occasionally striped, with green or
bronze foliage; **'Fordhook Giant,'**
a white-stemmed heirloom;
'Gazelle,' which produces a contrast
of dark green leaves with deep red
stems and veins, all in 58 days;
'Lucullus,' with light green, incredibly crumpled, curly leaves and
broad stems with rounded, white ribs;
'Orange Fantasia,' with orange stems;
'Perpetual,' a heat-resistant, non-
bolting cultivar with small, pale green
stems and spinach-like leaves; **'Rainbow,'** with a combination of red, orange,
yellow or white stems; **'Rhubarb,'** with
bright red stems; and **'Silverado,'**
with creamy white stems.

Problems and Pests

Rare problems with downy mildew,
powdery mildew, leaf miners, aphids,
caterpillars and root rot can occur.

*If you find that chard fades out in your
garden during the heat of summer,
you can plant a second crop in mid-
summer for fresh leaves in late summer
and fall.*

'Bright Lights'

Corn

Zea

Corn is believed to have originated in South America. Widely grown by native peoples in both North and South America, corn is one of the "three sisters" of native gardens: corn, beans and squash. All three were grown together as companions. The beans fixed nitrogen in the soil and could climb up the corn for support. The large leaves of squash shaded the soil and kept weeds to a minimum.

Starting

Start seed directly in the garden once the last frost date has passed and the soil has warmed; seed will rot in too cool a soil. Depending on the variety you choose, corn can take from 75 to 110 days to mature. If your growing season is short or the soil is slow to warm, you may prefer to start your corn 4–6 weeks early in peat pots and transplant it to the garden after the last frost date.

Avoid growing both popcorn and sweet corn, or keep them well separated, to avoid cross-pollination, which can make both of them inedible.

Growing

Corn grows best in **full sun**. The soil should be **fertile, moist** and **well drained**. As the plant develops, you can mound more soil around its base; the stem will develop roots in this soil, and the plant will be stronger and less likely to blow over in a strong wind.

Resist the temptation to remove the tassels at the top of the plant. The tassels serve an important purpose, as they are the male portion of the plant, which supplies the pollen. The fine, yellow dust (pollen) shed

by the tassels falls onto the silk of the cob, which is the female portion of the plant. Each silk thread is attached to a kernel. If no pollen falls onto the silk, no kernel will form. Shaking the plants when the pollen is being shed can help increase pollination.

Harvesting

Corn is ready to pick when the silks start to turn brown and the kernels are plump. If you peel the husk back just slightly, you will be able to see if the kernels are plump.

Use heirloom varieties as quickly as possible after picking because they begin to turn starchy as soon as they are picked. Newer selections have had their genes modified to increase their sweetness and ability to stay sweet after picking. These varieties can be stored for a while with no loss of sweetness.

Tips

Corn is an architectural grass that looks similar to some of the upright ornamental grasses, such as miscanthus. Plant it in groups of 5–9 in your beds and borders. Also, because corn is wind pollinated, plants need to be fairly close together for pollination to occur. Planting it in groups rather than rows improves your pollination rates when you are growing only a few plants.

To ensure maximum sweetness, cobs should be immersed in ice cold water as soon as possible after picking, and left in the water until cooked. Keep the cobs out of the hot sun as much as possible. These two steps are vital because the sugars in the kernels quickly convert to starches after the cobs are harvested, producing a less sweet product.

Recommended

Z. mays is a sturdy, upright grass with bright green leaves with undulating edges. Plants grow 1.2–2.4 m tall and spread 30–60 cm. **Var. *rugosa*** (sweet corn) matures in 65–80 days and falls into several sweetness categories that gauge both how sweet the corn is and how quickly the sugar turns to starch once the corn is picked. Some of the sweeter corns are less tolerant of cold soils. Kernels can be white or yellow, or cobs may have a combination of both colours. For fun, **var. *praecox*** (popcorn) matures in 100–110 days and has shorter cobs with hard, yellow, white or red kernels.

One could write an entire book on nothing but corn, because there are so many different varieties, but I'll narrow it down to just a few here based on their unique and fine qualities. **Mirai Series** is a group of hybrids regarded as one of the most delicious corn series available. '**Mirai Yellow**' is ready in 75 days, bearing succulent cobs 15 cm long with super tender, sweet corn. '**Mirai Bicolor**' produces cobs 20 cm long with golden yellow, tender, sweet kernels, with the occasional white kernel thrown in. '**Mirai White**' is an albino form, bearing extra-tender, sweet, white cobs with kernels to the tip.

Sugar-enhanced selections are also very popular, and the description likely says it all. '**Buttergold**' is ready for harvest in 63 days and was bred for northern climates. This early, all-yellow selection produces cobs 20 cm long with excellent flavour. '**Frisky**' is a sugary corn with tender and creamy, bicoloured cobs. By comparison, '**Early Sunglow**' is a normal sugar corn, bearing extra-early, bright yellow cobs. This classic variety is ideal for cold-weather planting and is often included with the first-sown seeds of the season. '**Honey 'n' Pearl**' is a super sweet variety, somewhere in between enhanced and normal.

Problems and Pests

Corn earworms, aphids, caterpillars, downy mildew, rust, smut and fungal leaf spots can cause problems for corn.

There are ornamental varieties of corn available; some, such as 'Fiesta' and 'Seneca Indian,' have colourful kernels; others, such as 'Harlequin' and 'Variegata,' have foliage striped in red, green and white or creamy white, respectively.

Cucumbers

Cucumis

Often people think that there is little in the way of nutrients in cucumbers. Another myth is that there are few ways to use this vegetable in our daily diet; however, if you browse through a vegetarian or vegan cookbook, you'll find that they're not only good for you but also versatile in the culinary arts…and straight from the garden, yummy!

Starting

Cucumbers can be started indoors about 4 weeks before the last frost date or can be sown directly into the garden once the last frost date has passed and the soil has warmed up. If you are starting your plants indoors, plant the seeds in peat pots so the roots will not be damaged or disturbed when you transplant them outdoors.

Growing

Cucumbers grow well in **full sun** or **light shade**. The soil should be **fertile, moist** and **well drained**. Consistent moisture is most important when plants are germinating and once fruit is being produced. If you are growing your cucumbers up a trellis or other support, you will probably need to tie the vines in place. Use strips of old nylons or other soft ties to avoid damaging the plants.

Harvesting

When to harvest will depend on the kind of cucumbers you are growing. Pickling cucumbers are picked while they are young and small. Slicing cucumbers can be picked when mature or when small if you want to use them for pickling. Long and slender Oriental cucumbers are picked when mature and tend to be sweeter, developing no bitter flavour with age.

Tips

Cucumbers are versatile trailing plants. They can be left to wind their way through the other plants in your garden or grown up trellises or other supports. The mound-forming varieties make attractive additions to container gardens.

Cucumbers keep producing fruit as long as you don't let the fruit stay on the vines for too long. Pick cucumbers as soon as they are a good size for eating. The more you pick, the more the plants will produce.

Recommended

C. sativus is a trailing annual vine with coarse leaves and bristly stems. It matures in 45–60 days. Popular slicing and salad cucumbers include the long, slender **'English Telegraph'** and **'Sweet Slender'**; All America Selections winner **'Fanfare,'** a prolific bush selection; and the high-yielding **'Stonewall.'** **'Armenian'** is an heirloom cucumber. This strong, vigorous grower is ready in 50–55 days, producing fruit with thin, light green skin resembling Asian varieties. **'Burpless'** is another slicing cucumber, ready in 62 days. It was bred for those who experience a bit of gassiness after eating cucumbers. This hybrid is mild and non-astringent, with a thin, tender skin— no peeling required, and no gas. **'Straight Eight'** is ready in 60 days and is considered to have superb

flavour compared to other selections. It produces mid-green, uniformly shaped, 20 cm long cucumbers.

Two highly recommended novelty cucumbers are **'Tondo di Manduria'** and **'Lemon.'** The first, native to Italy, is ready in 60–70 days and produces rounded fruits about the size of a lemon, lightly striped with dark and light green. If left to grow larger, the fruit can be treated similar to a melon. With low sugar levels, this cucumber is ideal for a diabetic diet. The second of the two is an heirloom variety, bearing 7 cm oval, bright yellow fruits on vigorous vines. This prolific cucumber has a slight lemon flavor and fragrance in late stages of development. **'Beit Alpha'** is a Lebanese type originating from the Middle East. It bears 15 cm long, smooth, medium green fruit with

'Lemon'

thin skin, similar to a garden cucumber. It is highly disease resistant and is ready in 55 days. **'Long White'** is ready in 85 days. This cucumber is not bitter and has a thin, tender, white skin, which removes the need for peeling. It has firm flesh with a sweet but tangy flavour.

Pickling cucumbers are harvested when small, and popular cultivars include the disease-tolerant, semi-bush **'Cross Country'** and the prolific, bushy **'Patio Pickles.'** One of the more highly recommended selections is **'Alibi,'** for its vigour and versatility; it is ready in only

'Alibi' (above)

50–55 days when picking for pickling purposes. The mature fruits can
reach 7–10 cm long but are more
often harvested at 5 cm for smoother
pickles. If picked regularly, they
should produce almost all season
long. **'Cool Breeze'** is unique because
almost all of the flowers will produce fruit, requiring no pollination.
In 50 days, this French Gourmet
cuke will be ready for harvest, at
10–12 cm long for the best flavour.

Problems and Pests

Problems with powdery mildew,
downy mildew, mosaic virus, white
flies, aphids, cucumber beetles, bacterial wilt, leaf spot, scab and ring
spot can occur.

Eggplants

Solanum

Eggplants are native to India and generally enjoy warmer weather than occurs naturally in most Ontario gardens. We can grow eggplants successfully by taking advantage of natural hot spots, varieties needing shorter seasons and heat-retaining mulch.

Starting

Seeds can be started indoors 6–8 weeks before the last frost date. Germination rates improve if bottom heat is used. Don't plant seedlings into the garden until the soil is warm and night temperatures stay above 15° C. Space seedlings 30–45 cm apart, unless your selection requires closer spacing; check the seed packet or plant tag.

Growing

Eggplants grow best in **full sun** in a warm, sheltered location. The soil should be **fertile, moist** and **well drained**. Pick the warmest spot in your garden to grow these plants. Dark mulch keeps the soil warmer and reduces evaporation from the soil. Mix compost into the soil to improve fertility and moisture retention.

Harvesting

Eggplants take 50–60 days to begin producing fruit, though they can take longer in cooler Canadian gardens. Choose the shorter-season varieties for the best yields. Cut fruit cleanly from the plants with a sharp knife to prevent damage.

Tips

Eggplants develop fruit in a variety of sizes, shapes and colours. Plant several types for an interesting display and so you can sample varieties you are less familiar with. Plants are bushy and bear pretty flowers, making them a welcome addition to beds and borders.

Recommended

S. melongena var. *esculentum* is a bushy plant with small, purple or white flowers. The fruit ranges in

shape from small and round to long and slender and in colour from deep purple to white, with mottled variations in between. Flavour varies significantly from cultivar to cultivar; experiment to see which ones grow best and which ones you enjoy the most. **'Baby Bell'** produces small, round, purple fruit. **'Cloud Nine'** produces pale creamy white fruit. **'Fairy Tale'** is an All America Selections winner with long, light purple, white-streaked fruit. **'Banka'** is early to set and produces even under poor seasonal conditions. Ready in 100 days, this eggplant produces heavily, bearing 7–8 large fruits per plant. The plant itself is relatively compact but is best staked for support. **'Orlando'** is ready in 85 days, bearing finger length, dark purple fruits that are bitter-free. The dwarf, 50 cm tall plants are ideal for

containers on a hot patio. An earlier variety, **'Baby Rosanna,'** bears golf ball–sized, bitter-free fruits on dwarf plants. Ideal for containers, this eggplant produces fruit that maintains its flavour, quality and colour well after being harvested. **'Birgah'** is a hybrid that produces large, heavy, dark purple, rounded fruits. The fruit is slightly ribbed, with white flesh and excellent flavour. **'Hansel'** bears elongated, purple fruits in clusters of 3–6, with very few seeds and great flavour. The fruit should be harvested at about 7 cm in length or longer. Ready in 55 days, this selection is great for containers or small spaces. **'Kermit'** is a green and white, Thai variety. Its compact form is well branched, supporting sets of rounded fruits 5 cm across.

Problems and Pests

Blister beetles, lace bugs, blight and potato beetles can cause problems.

Eggplants were slow to catch on in the West after being discovered in Asia, possibly because of their nickname "mad apple" and their reputation for causing insanity.

Eggplants are best grown in zone 5; however, they can be successfully grown in zones 3 and 4 if given a head start indoors and extra protection outdoors.

Fennel

Foeniculum

Fennel has been part of history for thousands of years in one capacity or another. Herbalists have touted its healing capabilities, and cooks have used fennel both as a vegetable and as a herb in a variety of ways. This plant even possesses cosmetic qualities and is said to smooth wrinkles and lines on the face as well as refresh tired eyes.

Fennel bulbs combine well with many other vegetables in savoury recipes but make an interesting addition to sweet recipes, too. Try adding some to your next fruit salad.

Starting

Seeds can be started directly in the garden around the last frost date or about 4 weeks earlier indoors.

Growing

Fennel grows best in **full sun**. The soil should be **average to fertile, moist** and **well drained**. Avoid planting fennel near dill or corian- der because cross-pollination reduces seed production and makes the seed flavour of each less distinct. Fennel easily self-sows.

Harvesting

Harvest fennel leaves as needed for fresh use. The seeds can be har- vested when ripe, in late summer

or fall. Shake the seedheads over a sheet to collect the seeds. Let them dry out before storing them.

Florence fennel can be harvested as soon as the bulbous base becomes swollen. Pull plants up as needed, and harvest any left in the ground at the end of the season before the first fall frost.

Tips

Fennel is an attractive addition to a mixed bed or border. The flowers attract pollinators and predatory insects to the garden.

Recommended

F. vulgare is a short-lived perennial that forms clumps of loose, feathery foliage. It grows 60 cm–1.8 m tall and spreads 30–60 cm. Clusters of small, yellow flowers are borne in late summer. The seeds ripen in fall. The species is primarily grown for its seeds and leaves. **Var.** *azoricum* (Florence fennel, finocchio) is a biennial that forms a large, edible bulb at the stem base. This variety is grown for its stem, leaves and bulb. The licorice-flavoured bulb is popular raw in salads, cooked in soups or stews or roasted like other root vegetables. '**Solaris**' is a large, uniform

selection, producing semi-flat bulbs that are vigorous and resistant to bolting. **'Zefa Fino'** is ready for harvest in 80 days, bolt resistant and very large. It bears flattish bulbs, green almost to the root. **'Orion'** is also ready in 80 days and has large, thick, rounded bulbs. It has a higher yield than open-pollinated varieties, a nice anise flavour and crisp texture. **Var.** *dulce* (sweet fennel) bears green-brown seeds. **'Purpureum'** ('Atropurpureum'; bronze fennel) is similar in appearance to the species but has bronzy purple foliage. This cultivar is usually sold as an ornamental, but its parts are entirely edible.

Problems and Pests

Fennel rarely suffers from any problems.

Florence fennel stems, or what are commonly referred to as the bulbs, are rather like celery, as they are formed by layered stems as opposed to complete layers like an onion.

Kale, Collards & Mustard Greens

Brassica

These nutrient-packed, leafy cabbage and broccoli siblings are some of the most decorative members of the Brassica family. This grouping is growing steadily in popularity, and for good reason. The nutrient content, flavour, texture and pure versatility are second to none. Mustards are most often eaten when quite young and lend a spicy flavour to stir-fries and salads. Collectively, this group is incredibly nutritious as well as delicious and is not just a garnish anymore.

Young, purple mustard greens

Starting

All three of these plants can be sown directly into the garden. They are all quite cold hardy and can be planted pretty much as soon as the soil can be worked in spring. A light frost won't harm them, though you should cover the young plants if nighttime temperatures are expected to drop to -10° C, or lower. You may wish to make several successive plantings of mustard because the leaves have the best flavour when they are young and tender.

Growing

These plants grow best in **full sun**. The soil should be **fertile, moist** and **well drained**. Mustard in particular should not be allowed to dry out, or the leaves may develop a bitter flavour.

Harvesting

Because the leaves are what you will be eating, you don't have to wait very long after planting to start harvesting. Once plants are established, you can start harvesting leaves as needed. Pick a few of the outer leaves from each plant.

Tips

These plants make a striking addition to beds and borders, where the foliage creates a good complement and backdrop for plants with brightly coloured flowers.

Recommended

B. oleracea var. *acephala* (collards; Scotch kale, curly-leaved kale) and *B. oleracea* var. *fimbriata* (Siberian kale, Russian kale) are the kales and collards; however, the two common names are not always used consistently.

Popular kale selections include the following. **'Blue Curled'** and **'Blue Ridge'** have good flavour and vigour. **'Improved Dwarf Siberian'** is ready in 50 days, maintaining its quality in the garden long after other selections have bolted. **'Winter Red'** produces dark green, oak-shaped leaves with purple veins. The tender, sweet leaves are ready in 50 days, reaching 60–75 cm in height. A series of kales incredibly popular for their mild, crisp flavour, colour variance, vigour and cold resistance includes **'Redbor,' 'Winterbor'** and **'Ripbor.'** They're early, high-yielding heirloom selections. **'Red Russian'** is also an heirloom. It produces tender, sweet, green leaves with red spines. **'Curly Green'** is as it's named—very curly, green and great even when flowering. **'Tuscan'** ('Black Tuscany,' 'Lacinato,' 'Dinosaur') is one of the tastiest forms of kale and is beautiful as an ornamental as well. It bears long, strap-like, blistered, dark green to almost black leaves.

Popular collards include **'Green Glaze,'** often referred to as "greasy greens." **'Top Bunch'** is a Georgia-type hybrid with large, slightly textured leaves, ready in 50 days. **'Flash'** is another early variety with smooth leaves. This selection is very slow to bolt and will continue to produce while the leaves are picked throughout the season. **'Hi-Crop'** has crinkled, blue-green, smooth leaves and a sweet flavour. This bolt-resistant variety is ready in 70 days. **'Blue Max'** is highly disease resistant and is ready in 70 days, while

Green and purple kale ready for harvest

'**Champion**' is ready in 60 days, bearing rich green leaves in a compact form.

B. juncea subsp. *rugosa* (mustard) forms large clumps of ruffled, creased or wrinkled leaves in shades of green, blue-green, bronze or purple. '**Savanna**' produces large, thick, deep green leaves with a savoury but mild flavour. '**Florida Broadleaf**' is an heirloom variety, producing smooth leaves with white midribs. Ready in 45–50 days, this mustard has a sharp cabbage flavour when leaves are harvested young. '**Mizuna**' ('Japonica') is a Japanese mustard variety with finely cut, curled leaves with a pleasant, mild flavour. Ready in 65 days, this selection will continue to grow after being cut. '**Mibuna**' has lance-shaped leaves, mild flavour and is regarded as a cold season vegetable. It is mature in 40 days, but the baby leaves can be harvested at 20 days. '**Red Giant**' produces brilliant maroon leaves with light green midribs. The leaves are spicy and flavourful and ready for harvest in 45 days.

Problems and Pests

Problems with cutworms, leaf miners, caterpillars, root maggots, cabbage white butterfly larvae, white rust, downy mildew and powdery mildew can occur.

Collards were some of the earliest cultivated forms of Brassica oleracea. *The Romans brought them to Britain in 400 BCE, where they became known as Coleworts. Unfortunately, they were often boiled beyond recognition and weren't really appreciated until much, much later in history.*

'Tuscan' kale (left); collards (right)

Kohlrabi

Brassica

The tender, swollen stem base of kohlrabi is curious looking, like something you'd imagine would be grown in a futuristic garden. But don't let its funny appearance put you off of this yummy vegetable. The leaf bases become stretched as the bulb forms, and new leaves continue to sprout from the top of the rounded bulb. See, nothing to fear. Let the experimentation begin!

Starting

Seeds can be sown directly in the garden approximately 30 cm apart around the last frost date. This plant matures quite quickly, so make several small sowings 1–2 weeks apart to have tender, young kohlrabi for most of summer.

Growing

Kohlrabi grows best in **full sun**. The soil should be **fertile, moist** and **well drained**, though plants adapt to most moist soils. Encourage good growth by keeping the soil moist, and harvest quickly once bulbs form.

Harvesting

Keep a close eye on your kohlrabi because the bulbs can become tough and woody quickly if left in the ground too long. The bulbs are

Kohlrabi is a cross between a cabbage and a turnip, something that tends to ward off those who like neither, but it's a combination made in heaven.

generally well rounded and 5–10 cm in diameter when ready for harvesting. Pull up the entire plant and cut just below the bulb. Then cut the leaves and stems off and compost them or use them to mulch the bed.

Tips

Low and bushy, with white or purple bulbs, kohlrabi makes an interesting edging plant for beds and borders and can be included in container gardens, particularly those in which you like to change the plantings regularly.

Recommended

B. oleracea subsp. *gongylodes* forms a low, bushy clump of blue-green foliage. As the plant matures, the stem just above ground level swells and becomes rounded. This is the edible part. **'Purple'** and **'White'** are common in seed catalogues and are the standard hybrids of the subspecies. They mature in 55 days, are very productive and are nutty in flavour without becoming woody.

More unique cultivars and hybrids are also available. **'Rapid Star'** bears rounded, pale green bulbs and is ready in 52 days. The **Vienna Series** includes **'White Vienna,'** which takes 56 days to produce light green to white bulbs with smooth skin and white flesh, and **'Purple Vienna,'** which is similar in every aspect but colour. This series is known for its sweet flavour and tender texture, and the bulbs are ideal for freezing for later use. **'Granlibakken'** is an earlier variety, ready in 46 days because of its vigour. It bears light green, uniform, rounded bulbs with an extra tender texture and super sweet flavour. **'Korridor'** is also an early selection, bearing white bulbs with a rich flavour. **'Kolibri'** is considered to be one of the best-tasting purple varieties, ready in 45 days.

Problems and Pests

Problems with cutworms, leaf miners, caterpillars, root maggots, cabbage white butterfly larvae, white rust, downy mildew and powdery mildew can occur.

Some people find this vegetable to be a magnet to insects that commonly frequent other Brassicas, but a floating row cover atop your crop will reduce that threat.

Leeks

Allium

Leeks can rival most ornamental grasses for garden presence. The plants are strongly upright with stunning dark blue-green leaves that arch from the main stem. Planted in a small group, they are a welcome addition to any border.

Starting

Leeks can be sown directly in the garden, but because they take quite a long time to mature, you may want to start them indoors 8–10 weeks before you plan to plant them outdoors. Once the stems reach the diameter of a pencil, transplant them to the garden, roughly 10–15 cm apart, in a trench 10 cm deep. To make transplanting easier, trim the roots by half; otherwise leave them intact.

Such a long time indoors can encourage lanky growth, so if you don't have supplemental lighting or a very bright window, you may find it better to purchase plants when you are ready to plant them outdoors.

Growing

Leeks grow best in **full sun**. The soil should be **fertile** and **well drained**, but plants adapt to most well-drained soils. Improve less-than-ideal soil by

The leek is the emblem of Wales, and Welsh people still wear one on their lapel on St. David's Day, March 1.

mixing in compost or adding a layer of compost mulch once you have planted. You can mound mulch, soil or straw up around the base of the plants as summer progresses to encourage tender, white growth low on the plant.

Don't feel you have to harvest all your leeks in fall. Some plants can be left in place to be harvested in spring or even left to flower and go to seed. These perennial plants will return year after year, and new seedlings can be allowed to grow in to replace fading plants.

Harvesting

Leeks can be harvested as soon as they are mature in early fall, but because they are so hardy, you can just harvest them as you need them until the ground begins to freeze. At that point you should pull up any you want for winter use.

Leeks keep for several weeks in the refrigerator if you cut the roots short and wrap the leeks in plastic. For longer storage, they can be frozen. Be sure to double bag them so the onion-like flavour doesn't seep into any other food you have in the freezer.

Tips

Leeks, with their bright blue-green leaves, are one of the most ornamental of all the onions. Plant them in groups in your beds and borders.

Recommended

A. ampeloprasum subsp. *porrum* is an upright perennial with blue-green leaves that cascade from the central stem. Globe-shaped clusters of flowers are borne atop a 90 cm tall stem the second year from planting. A wide array of hybrids and cultivars is available. **'Monstrous Carentan'** is a hardy, vigorous leek that is sweet, mild and very cold tolerant. It is ready in roughly 110 days. **'Lancelot'** is ready in 90 days, producing bluish, erect foliage with bright white stalks that can reach up to 25 cm in height. This selection can be sown tightly together, without thinning, for a summer harvest of smaller, tender baby leeks. **'Maine'** is a semi-erect plant, ready in 117 days, producing blue-green foliage. This selection was bred for its cold tolerance and was adapted for a fall harvest, as opposed to a summer harvest. **'American Flag'** ('Broad London') is a mild leek, sweeter than onions. It grows to only 15 cm tall, matures very firm and is ready in 115 days. **'King**

Richard' is an early variety, producing large leeks with white stems over 30 cm tall to the first leaf in only 75 days. This variety is not hardy enough for overwintering but can withstand a medium to heavy frost without losing its texture or flavour. **'Lincoln'** is a baby bunching variety, ready in 50 days, bearing tall, slender scallion-like leeks that are sweet and tender. **'Bandit'** is a very winter-hardy leek bearing dark blue-green, erect leaves, ready in 120 days, with good uniformity, a thick shaft and a little bulbing at soil level.

Problems and Pests

Problems with rot, mildew, smut, rust, leaf spot, onion flies and thrips can occur.

Leeks were once a popular cure for venomous bites, ulcers, nosebleeds, poor eyesight, drunkenness, toothaches, coughs, headaches and many other ills.

Lettuce & Mesclun

Letuca

Lettuce, with its undulating or rippled edges and variable leaf colours, is an ornamental treasure trove that deserves a spot in the garden even if you don't care for salad. Mesclun, whether a spicy or a mild blend, makes a welcome addition to salads and stir-fries while providing a good groundcover in the garden.

Starting

Lettuce and mesclun can be started directly in the garden around the last frost date. The seeds of leafy lettuces and mesclun can be scattered across a prepared area and do not have to be planted in rows, but you may wish to be more selective when planting head lettuces so you don't have to thin the plants out as much later.

If you make several smaller plantings spaced 1–2 weeks apart, you won't end up with more plants than you can use maturing at once. For an earlier crop, start a few plants indoors about 4 weeks before you plan to plant them outdoors.

Growing

Lettuce and mesclun grow well in **full sun, light shade** or **partial shade** in a sheltered location. The soil should be **fertile, moist** and **well drained**. Add plenty of compost to improve the soil, and be sure to keep your lettuce moist. Lettuce is very prone to drying out in hot and windy situations, so it is best to plant it where it will get some protection. Plants under too much stress can quickly bolt and go to seed or simply wilt and die.

Harvesting

Head-forming lettuce can be harvested once the head is plump. If the weather turns very hot, you may wish to cut heads earlier because the leaves develop a bitter flavour once the plants go to flower.

Loose-leaf lettuce and mesclun can be harvested by pulling a few leaves off as needed or by cutting an entire plant 5–10 cm above ground level. Most will continue to produce new leaves even if cut this way.

Tips

Lettuce and mesclun make interesting additions to container plantings, either alone or combined with other plants. In beds and borders, mesclun makes a decorative edging plant. All lettuces and mesclun are fairly low growing and should be planted near the front of a border so they will be easier to get to for casual picking.

Each Canadian consumes on average 12 kg of lettuce annually.

Recommended

L. sativa forms a clump of ruffle-edged leaves and comes in many forms.

Loose-leaf lettuce forms a loose rosette of leaves rather than a central head. A few of the many recommended loose-leaf varieties include the following. **'Grand Rapids'** is ready in 45 days, producing large, frilly, bright green leaves that are tender and sweet. This variety is vigorous and slower to bolt than its contemporaries. **'Prizehead'** produces loose, crumpled leaves edged with reddish brown in 45–55 days and has a buttery flavour. **'Red Salad Bowl'** produces loose, deeply cut, deep burgundy leaves in a rosette form and is slow to bolt. The flavour is mild and non-bitter. **'Simpson Elite'** is mature at 50 days but can be harvested at 30–45 days. It is

To add a twist to your purchased mesclun mixes, try adding a few herb seeds; cilantro, dill, parsley and basil are a few you may enjoy.

incredibly vigorous, with a delicate flavour that rarely gets bitter. **'New Red Fire'** produces ruby red leaves in a loose form. It has a sweet flavour and proven bolt resistance.

Butterhead or Boston lettuce forms a loose head and has a very mild flavour. **'Bibb'** produces a loose head of buttery leaves with a distinctive flavour. This selection is early, maturing in 57 days, so start it early to avoid it bolting in hot summer weather. **'Esmeralda'** is considered a gourmet lettuce. It has a sweet flavour and succulent texture and is resistant to bolting and pests. **'Yugoslavian Red Butterhead'** is an heirloom variety bearing 30 cm wide heads covered in red-tinged outer leaves surrounding an almost white centre, with a mild flavour.

Romaine or cos lettuce has a more upright habit, and the heads are fairly loose but cylindrical in shape.

'**Baby Star**' is a mini romaine that is ready in 65–85 days, producing dark green, shiny leaves with a creamy white blanched heart.

Crisphead or iceberg lettuce forms a very tight head of leaves and includes the following varieties. '**Early Great Lakes**' is ready in 65–85 days, depending on whether you choose to harvest baby leaves or fully mature ones. This variety has bright green outer leaves and creamy white inner leaves. '**Ithaca**' is a very popular head lettuce, producing tightly wrapped, crisp heads with great vigour. '**Summertime**' is a later iceberg-type lettuce, compact overall and slow to become bitter.

Mesclun mixes can be a combination of different lettuces, usually loose-leaf types, eaten while very young and tender. Mixes often also include other species of plants, including mustard, broccoli, radicchio, endive, arugula, chicory and spinach. Most seed catalogues offer a good selection of pre-mixed mesclun as well as separate selections to create your own mix. The mixes are often ready in 40–65 days, in balanced blends of spicy, mild and sweet. The colour and texture of the leaves are quite varied, making for a beautiful salad.

Problems and Pests

Problems with root rot, leaf spot, flea beetle and mosaic virus can occur.

An essential tip for successful lettuce from the garden is to use a floating row cover for protection against pests and, in some cases, tip burn in the hot summer sun.

Okra

Abelmoschus

Okra is grown with variable success throughout parts of Canada, including southern Ontario. Some gardeners have great success, while others are often disappointed. Started early indoors to extend the season, okra will have more of a chance to mature. When it is time to plant it in the garden, hope for a long, hot summer and you will end up with either baby or mature okra. Either way, it's delicious in soups and stews and fun to grow.

Starting

Okra germinates quickly in warm soil. Seeds should be soaked overnight before planting. Start them in peat pots 6–8 weeks before you plan to move them to the garden. Wait until the last frost date has passed and the soil has warmed before moving them outside.

Growing

Okra grows best in **full sun** in a sheltered location. The soil should be **fertile, moist** and **well drained**. Okra likes hot growing conditions, so plant it in the hottest part of your garden, and use plenty of mulch to conserve water.

Harvesting

This plant can be spiny, so it is best to wear gloves when harvesting the fruit. Pick the fruit when it is still immature, usually 1–2 weeks after the flower drops and the pod sets. Pods are usually harvested when they are 8–10 cm long.

Tips

Okra makes an attractive addition to container plantings, with the added bonus that you can extend your growing season by bringing the entire container indoors when cool weather or frost is expected.

Recommended

A. esculentus is a bushy, upright plant with sometimes spiny foliage and brown- or purple-spotted, yellow, hibiscus-like flowers. Flowers are borne at the base of each leaf.

'Cajun Delight' (below)

The red stems and upright form are quite stunning mixed in with ornamental plants.

Okra is a love-it or hate-it type of vegetable. It has a slimy texture when cooked, and a flavour described as "a mix between green beans and oysters," but it's fun to try something new, both in the garden and in the kitchen.

Plants mature about 50 days after being transplanted but require plenty of hot weather to flower and fruit. **'Cajun Delight'** and **'Dwarf Green'** are two of the more common varieties available. **'Red Burgundy,'** a 2010 All America Selections winner, is ready in 85 days, bearing deep red stems, branches and leaf midribs. The fruits grow 15–20 cm long when mature, resulting in tender pods that turn a deep green when cooked. **'Clemson Spineless,'** also an AAS winner, is ready in 56 days, producing tender, rich green pods 15 cm long. The pods are pointed and slightly grooved. **'Millionaire'** is an early hybrid, perfect for Ontario gardens; medium, sturdy plants yield dark green pods. The pods should be harvested when they reach 8–10 cm in length. The large flowers produced before the fruits are robust

and edible, similar to squash flowers. They too can be stuffed with rice or meat mixtures, or used as a yummy garnish. **'Annie Oakley'** is earlier yet, ready in 45 days, but spinier than most. This is a great cultivar for northern Ontario. **'Blondy'** is mature at 48 days in an open-pollinated form. It grows into a compact, 90 cm tall plant, bearing heaps of pods. It was bred for northern climates and is another AAS winner.

Problems and Pests

Occasional problems with slugs, spider mites, whiteflies, cabbage white butterfly larvae, fungal leaf spot or powdery mildew can occur.

Using heat-conserving techniques in the garden to heat things up for okra is of great benefit. Cloches, tents and floating row covers to trap heat are all recommended.

Onions

Allium

Onions are one of the oldest cultivated plants, having been grown for over 5000 years. They have been cultivated for so long that their country of origin is not even known. It is known, however, that the ancient Greeks, Romans and Egyptians all grew and ate onions in great abundance. The onion's popularity has not waned, as an average of 9 kg per person in Canada is consumed annually. That's a lot to say for a vegetable that makes our eyes tear up and leaves us with bad breath.

Starting

Onions can be started from seed indoors 6–8 weeks before you plan to plant them outdoors; they can also be sown directly in the garden once the last frost date has passed. When sowing onion seed, place 2–3 seeds per 2.5 cm in rows 1 cm deep. Thin the seedlings once they're approximately 5 cm tall, leaving a seedling every 2.5–5 cm. The onions you pulled can be used as green onions, or scallions. If you don't want to start from seed, sets of starter onions can be purchased and planted in spring.

Bunching onions are usually started from seed sown directly in the garden. They are quick to mature, so make several smaller sowings 2–3 weeks apart from spring to mid-summer for a regular supply.

Onions make interesting additions to container plantings, particularly close to the house if you just want to pick a few leaves at a time.

"Knowing your onions" is an old phrase referring to the more than 400 Allium species, including leeks, chives, garlic, shallots and many forms of onion.

Growing

Onions should be grown in **full sun**. The soil should be **fertile, moist** and **well drained**. Onions use plenty of water but will rot in very wet soil. They are poor at competing with other plants, so keep them well weeded. A good layer of mulch will conserve moisture and keep the weeds down. Be sure to water during periods of extended drought.

Harvesting

All onions can be harvested and used as needed throughout the season. For green onions, pull up onions that need thinning, or just pinch back the tops if you want the bulbs to mature or the plant to continue to produce leaves.

Bulb onions grown for storage are ready to be harvested when the leaves begin to yellow and flop over and the shoulders of the bulbs are just visible above the soil line. They should be pulled up and allowed to dry for a few days before being stored in a dry, cold, frost-free spot.

Onions are perennials and can also be left in the ground over winter, though the flavour can become quite strong the second year. They will flower the second summer.

Tips

Onions have fascinating cylindrical leaves that add an interesting vertical accent to the garden. Include them in beds and borders, but if you want big bulbs, don't overly crowd them with other plants. Smaller bulbs form on plants that are too crowded, which is not a bad thing if you only want small bulbs.

Recommended

A. cepa (bulb onion) forms a clump of cylindrical foliage and develops

'Evergreen' (above)

a large, round or flattened bulb. Bulb formation is day-length dependent. Gardeners in Ontario tend to use northern onion varieties that have been developed for long days. Bulb formation begins when days are 15–16 hours long. There is a myriad of varieties to choose from, in a variety of sizes, colours, flavours and textures, but here are a handful that are tried-and-true and others to shake things up a bit. **'Candy'** is an extra-early seed onion that will grow just about anywhere. It bears large, mildly sweet bulbs in 85 days. The harvest can last until March if cured and stored properly. **'Redwing'** is an ultra reliable performer, ready in 100–120 days and a great keeper. It produces white, 7–8 cm diameter onions with deep maroon skins. **'Walla Walla'** is a traditional selection, known by most vegetable gardeners for good reason. It produces mild, sweet, large, flattened globes with golden skins. Ready in

125 days, this selection is not a good keeper, so grow only a few and use them immediately after harvest. **'Sweet Spanish'** is another well-known onion, bearing yellow-fleshed, sweet, mild bulbs in 110–115 days. It is a great keeper. **'Mount Witney'** is a Spanish variety, bearing jumbo-sized, juicy, sweet, mild onions. **'Red Bull'** is,

well, red. It maintains its dark red colour almost to its centre. The strong skin ensures its life in the pantry, and it's ready in 118 days. **'Champlain'** is an early bulb onion, maturing in 92 days. It is medium-sized with a strong skin that helps it to keep for long periods, and it is juicy and flavourful. **'Cowboy'** is a large onion, ready in mid-season, deliciously

sweet and mild, but not a great keeper. **'Talon'** is a large onion, ready closer to the end of the growing season, with high yields, good uniformity and excellent storage capability.

A. fistulosum (bunching onion, green onion, scallion) is a perennial that forms a clump of foliage. The plant quickly begins to divide and multiply from the base. Plants may develop small bulbs or no bulbs at all. Once established, these plants will provide you with green onions all spring and summer. **'Evergreen'** is ready in 60–75 days. This selection was bred for its crisp, deep green, rich, mild-tasting foliage. For something a little different, **'Salad Apache'** is a deep purple variety bearing deep purple-red–skinned ends in 80 days. The flavour is mild, and the texture is crisp. The purple outer skin blends with shades of silver when peeled, adding contrast and a little colour to your cooking. This is a great bunching onion to grow in containers. **'Red Baron'** is a later bunching onion, ready in 105–115 days. It produces high yields of intense red and green roots and thrives in high-density plantings.

A. oschaninii and *A. ascalonicum* are the two species of perennials known as shallots. *A. oschaninii* is considered to be the "true" shallot species that comes from Central to Southwest Asia. *A. ascalonicum* is more of an Indian species, equally as common and delicious. Like garlic, shallots are formed in offsets, or clusters making up a head of multiple cloves. The skin colour ranges from golden brown to rosy red to grey, and the white flesh can be tinged with green or pink. Shallots are firm and sweeter than other onions, yet pungent. They are also smaller—much smaller than a bulb onion but larger than the root end of a scallion. **'Banana'** is an unusual, long shallot with shiny, copper-brown skin, crisp, white flesh and a very distinctive flavour, ready in 85 days. **'Picador'** is a rounded shallot with brownish pink skin, white flesh tinged with pink and a unique, mild flavour, ready in 88 days. This selection is considered to be a French shallot.

Problems and Pests

Problems with smut, onion maggots and rot can occur.

Pearl onions are relatively unknown but delicious and fun to grow. 'Crystal Wax' is a popular variety, bearing tiny bulbs with a mild flavour, and is ideal for pickling.

Parsnips

Pastinaca

Despite needing a fairly long season to mature, parsnips
are well suited to northern gardens because they are best
eaten once they have had a few goods frosts to
sweeten their roots.

Starting

Sow seeds directly into the garden
as soon as the soil can be worked.
Be sure to keep the soil moist to
ensure good germination. Seeds
can be slow to germinate, sometimes taking up to 3 weeks, so mark
the location where you plant them.

Growing

Parsnips grow best in **full sun** but
tolerate some light shade. The soil
should be of **average fertility, moist**
and **well drained**. Be sure to work
the soil well and mix in compost to
improve the texture. Roots develop
poorly in heavy soil. Mulch to suppress weed growth and to conserve
moisture. Unlike carrots, parsnip
tops are very big and spreading, so
they take up a lot of room.

To avoid "hairy roots," do not use
manure as a fertilizer. However,
a bed that has manure in it from
the previous year should grow
good parsnips in the current year.

Harvesting

The roots can be pulled up in fall,
after the first few frosts, and stored,
like carrots, in damp sand in a cold,
frost-free location for up to 6 months.
Parsnips can also be mulched with
straw and pulled up in spring,
before they sprout new growth.
Frost improves the flavour because
some of the root starches are con-
verted to sugar in freezing weather.

Tips

Not the most ornamental of vegetables, parsnips provide a dark, leafy

*Roasting the roots brings out their
sweetness. Combine parsnips with
potatoes, carrots and other root
vegetables, then drizzle with oil and
sprinkle with herbs before roasting
for an hour, or until the vegetables
are tender.*

Parsnips can be pulled from the garden all winter in areas where the ground does not freeze into a solid, impenetrable mass.

background to low-growing plants and produce plenty of vegetables for very little effort.

Recommended

P. sativa is an upright plant with dark green, divided leaves. It develops a long, pale creamy yellow root that looks like a carrot. **'Andover,' 'Harris Model'** and **'Hollow Crown'** are commonly available cultivars. **'Javelin'** is a smooth-skinned parsnip that is resistant to canker. The uniform roots have great flavour, and the roots keep well in the soil for fall and winter harvest. **'Excalibur'** is a later variety, ready in 180 days. It produces smooth, almost bleached white roots with creamy flesh and sweet flavour. The roots have shallow crowns, which is great for later crops. **'Gladiator'** is considered to be the best hybrid parsnip for its consistently high quality,

silky smooth skin and true parsnip flavour. **'Arrow'** is an earlier variety producing large, uniform roots in great abundance with a sweet, delicate flavour and tender texture. **'Tender & True'** is an heirloom variety ready in 105 days. It is an open-pollinated parsnip, bearing long, canker-resistant roots.

Problems and Pests

Canker, carrot rust flies and onion maggots can affect parsnips.

This cousin of the carrot was once prescribed as a treatment for ulcers, colic, pain, consumption, snakebites and psychological ills.

Peas

Pisum

There is no replacement for picking peas straight from the vine, on a summer's day in the garden, and eating the peas straight from the pod with your feet firmly planted in the soil. The flavour is far superior to any pea you can buy in the store—fresh is best. Chances are that if you spent any time in the garden as a child, you remember picking, shelling and eating fresh peas straight from the pod, and why stop that tradition now?

Starting

Peas show an admirable apprecia-tion for cool spring weather and can be sown directly outdoors as soon as the soil can be worked and has dried out a bit. The seeds can rot in cold, wet soil, but a light frost or two won't do them any harm, and the sooner they are planted, the sooner you can begin eating peas.

Peas, like beans, can be treated with bacterial inoculant before planting to ensure a good supply of nitrogen-fixing bacteria on the roots.

Growing

Peas grow well in **full sun**. The soil should be **average to fertile, humus rich, moist** and **well drained**. Peas can grow a wide range of heights, but all benefit from a support of some kind to climb up. They develop small tendrils that twine around twiggy branches, nets or chain-link fences. Base your support height on the expected height of the plants, and make sure it is in place before your seeds sprout because the roots are quite shallow and can be dam-aged easily.

There are many peas to choose from. When deciding which kind to grow, think about the type of peas you will get the most use from. Then choose the mature plant height that is most suitable for the space you have.

Harvesting

Peas should be harvested when they are still young and tender. They can be pulled from the vine by hand, but use both hands—one to hold the

Snap peas

plant and one to pull the pea pod—to avoid damaging the plant. The more you pick, the more peas the plants will produce.

Peas have been cultivated for so many generations that their birthplace is unknown. There is, however, a legend that states that peas came from Thor, the Norse god of thunder. It was said that Thor sent peas crashing to the earth to plug up humans' wells, but a few missed the mark and rooted instead.

Smooth-seeded varieties are more starchy and are used for soups, while wrinkled varieties are sweeter and generally eaten fresh.

Tips

Peas are excellent plants for growing up a low chain-link fence, and the taller varieties create a privacy screen quite quickly. The shorter and medium-height peas make interesting additions to hanging baskets and container plantings. They can grow up the hangers or supports or can be encouraged to spill over the edges and trail down.

Recommended

P. sativum var. *sativum* is a climbing plant with bright green, waxy stems and leaves and white flowers. The resulting pods are grouped into three categories: shelling (English, garden) peas, snow (sugar) peas and snap (sugar snap) peas. The seeds are removed from the pods of shelling peas and are the only part eaten. Snow peas are eaten as flat, almost seedless pods, often including the edible vine tips and newest leaves.

Snap peas develop fat seeds, and the pod and seeds are eaten together. There is a wide array of varieties to choose from, but here are a few from each category.

Shelling pea varieties include the following. **'Alaska'** is one of the oldest peas available. It is a heavy producer, bearing 5–8 cm long pods in 50–55 days, and is resistant to cold, pests and wilt. **'Early Freezer'** is ready in 58 days, bearing double-podded peas, ranging from 7–8 peas in each 8 cm long pod. **'Green Arrow'** is an heirloom shelling pea, boasting high yields, 10 cm long pods and an average of 9–11 peas per pod. This tender pea requires no support, is ready in 58–63 days and is highly disease tolerant. **'Paladio'** produces big, easy-to-open pods. This variety is often borne in doubles, making for easy picking and shelling.

Snow peas are equally as varied. **'Snow Green'** has dark green, 8 cm long pods that are borne in multiples. The plants do not need support and are resistant to disease. **'Mammoth Melting'** is an heirloom variety that produces huge, long, edible pods with a sweet, mild flavour. **'Oregon Sugar Pod II'** is a heavy yielder, producing tender, flat, 10 cm long pods. This dwarf plant produces peas ready for harvest in 60 days. **'Oregon Giant'** is very similar but

is more uniform, with larger pods overall, and takes a little longer to mature.

For snap, or sugar snap, I'd recommend the following. **'Sugar Ann'** is an All America Selections winner and is ready for harvest in 75 days. It bears rounded, fleshy pods on vines that can reach up to 90 cm tall. **'Sugar Lace'** is self-supporting, only 40 cm tall with 8 cm long pods in a sweet and stringless form. **'Sugar Snap Cascadia'** is a dwarf variety ready for harvest in 70 days, bearing fleshy, crisp, sweet, rounded pods that remain tender and sweet for a long period, particularly compared to other varieties. It is also resistant to pea wilt.

Problems and Pests

Peas are somewhat prone to powdery mildew, so choose mildew-resistant varieties and avoid touching the plants when they are wet to prevent the spread of disease. Aphids and whiteflies can also cause problems.

Peppers

Capsicum

The variety of sweet and chili peppers is nothing short of remarkable. Among the many different shapes, colours and flavours of peppers, there is sure to be one or two that appeal to you. A cool summer can really put a damper on fruiting, which can make hot pepper growing, in particular, a bit tricky in Ontario gardens.

'Habanero' (above)

Starting

Peppers need warmth to germinate and grow, and they take a while to mature, so it is best to start them indoors 6–10 weeks before the last frost date. If you don't have ideal light conditions, your seedlings may become stretched out and do poorly even when moved to the garden. In this case, you may prefer to purchase started plants; many varieties are available at garden centres and nurseries.

Growing

Peppers grow best in **full sun** in a warm location. The soil should be **average to fertile, moist** and **well drained**. Mulch to ensure the soil stays moist because most Canadians need to plant their peppers in a fairly hot garden location.

Most gardens will be hot enough to grow sweet peppers, but chili

Pepper breeding is an incredibly competitive industry. Breeders from all over the world continue to try to produce the hottest pepper ever, even beyond what is currently the hottest, the 'Naga Jolokia.'

Peppers may be rated on a scale of 1–10 or by Scoville units. Sweet peppers have about 100 Scoville units, while habaneros can have up to 350,000 Scoville units.

peppers need hotter weather to bear fruit. Try a dark mulch in a hot spot if you've had little luck with these peppers in the past.

Harvesting

Peppers can be picked as needed, once they are ripe. Chili peppers can also be dried for use in winter.

Tips

Pepper plants are neat and bushy. Once the peppers set and begin to ripen, the plants can be very colourful as the bright red, orange and yellow fruits contrast beautifully with the dark green foliage. They are a worthwhile addition to a hot, sunny border, even if you don't care to eat peppers.

All peppers are good additions to container plantings. Chili peppers in particular are useful in containers because they usually have the most interesting fruit shapes, and the containers can be moved indoors or to a sheltered spot to extend the season if needed. Some of the smaller chili peppers also make interesting houseplants for warm, sunny windows.

Recommended

C. annuum is the most common species of sweet and hot peppers. Plants are bushy with dark green foliage. Flowers are white, and peppers can be shades of green, red, orange, yellow, purple or brown.

Cultivars of sweet peppers include **'Blushing Beauty,' 'Carmen,' 'Earlibird'** and **'Orange Sun.'** Some of the most tasty and beautiful sweet peppers are those in the **Fluo Series**, including: **'Fluo Lilac'** ('Early Lilac'), bearing grape purple, large bell peppers, sweet in flavour and firm in texture; and **'Fluo Orange,'** very similar but with a bright orange skin. **'Mini Belle'** is a mix commonly found in seed catalogues. The varieties that make up this mix are ready in 90 days on dwarf, compact plants that produce large yields of small, blocky, sweet bell peppers in red, orange, purple or brown. This mix is ideal for containers. **'Big Bertha'** is a sweet bell pepper that produces jumbo fruits that change from green to red with maturity. **'California Wonder'** bears crisp, thick-fleshed fruits with a mild, pleasant flavour.

Cultivars of chili peppers include **'Anaheim,'** **'Cayenne,'** **'Jalapeno,'** **'Scotch Bonnet'** and **'Thai,'** just to name a few.

Sweet banana peppers, or Hungarian wax peppers, are another group, more sweet than hot. They are elongated, often in bright shades of yellow and orange. **'Banana'** is an All America Selections winner ready in 70 days and is sweet, with no trace of heat. It can be harvested at any size but is best at 15–17 cm long. The fruits are pale yellow when ripe and are vigorously produced.

C. chinense **'Habanero'** is one of the hottest chili peppers. It is native to the Caribbean. **'Naga Jolokia'** ('Bhut Jolokia') is believed to be the world's hottest pepper. It is ready for harvest in 150 days, has Indian origins and is best sown indoors 8–10 weeks before the last frost to ensure fruit. **'Naga**

Jolokia Chocolate'** is similar but is dark reddish brown with a slightly mottled or rough-textured skin.

Problems and Pests

Rare problems with aphids and whiteflies can occur.

Capsaicin is the chemical that gives peppers their heat. It is also the chemical used in pepper spray.

Potatoes

Solanum

Potatoes were cultivated in South America for centuries before they were introduced to Europe by the Spanish. They were only introduced to North America after European immigrants brought them here. Today, heirloom varieties are in fashion, mixing it up with newer cultivars fancy and plain, small and large; no matter what new varieties come out, the heirloom potatoes are often the best and have stood the test of time.

Hill up the soil at the base of the plants as the potatoes mature to block out any light.

Starting

Sets of seed potatoes (small tubers) can be purchased and planted in spring a few weeks before the last frost date, as long as the soil isn't too cold and wet. Young plants can tolerate a light frost, but not a hard freeze. The seed potatoes can be cut into smaller pieces, as long as each one has an "eye," the dimpled spot from which the plant and roots grow. Each piece needs 30–45 cm of space around it to grow.

Growing

Potatoes prefer **full sun** but tolerate some shade. The soil should be **fertile, humus rich, acidic, moist** and **well drained**, though potatoes adapt to most growing conditions and tolerate both hot and cold weather. Mound soil up around the plants to keep the tubers out of the light as they develop.

All parts of the potato plant are poisonous except the tubers, and they can become poisonous if they are exposed to light. Green flesh is a good indication that your potatoes have been exposed to light. To protect your potatoes, mound soil around the plants, 2.5 cm or so per week, from mid-summer to fall. A straw mulch also effectively shades the developing tubers.

'Tolaas'

Is your potato high or low in starch? To find out, cut one in half, rub the cut surfaces together and then stick them to one another, like you were putting them back together. If they stick, the starch content is high. High-starch varieties are better for baking and mashing. Low-starch spuds are better for boiling and for potato salad.

'Chaleur' (below)

Harvesting

The tubers begin to form around the same time the plants begin to flower, usually sometime in August. You can dig up a few tubers at a time from this point on as you need them.

The remaining crop should be dug up in fall once the plants have withered, but before the first hard frost. Let them dry for a few hours on the soil, and then brush the dirt off and store the tubers in a cold, dark place. You can even save a few of the smaller tubers for planting the following spring.

Tips

These large, bushy plants with white, pink or light purple flowers are good filler plants for an immature border and are excellent at breaking up the soil in newer gardens.

Recommended

S. tuberosum is a bushy, mound-forming plant. It bears tiny, exotic-looking, white, pink or light purple flowers in late summer. There are many varieties of potatoes available. They can have rough or smooth, white, yellow, brown, red or blue skin and white, yellow, purple or blue flesh. A few popular varieties include **'All-Blue,'** with smooth, blue skin and light purple-blue flesh; **'Irish Cobbler,'** an heirloom with smooth, brown skin and white flesh that is widely adapted to extreme temperatures; **'Norland,'** with smooth, red skin and white flesh;

'Chieftan' (above)

Purchase seed sets of a variety that interests you rather than trying to grow potatoes bought from the grocery store. Potatoes from the store may have been treated to prevent sprouting, or they may be poorly suited to grow where you live.

and **'Yukon Gold,'** with smooth, light beige skin and yellow flesh.

Beyond the more traditional, well-known varieties are some of the more unusual and fun ones. **'Chaleur'** is a high-yielding, early Canadian variety with great tolerance to hot and dry conditions that bears large tubers. **'Kennebec'** is slowly on its way to becoming a commonly known spud because of its high yield potential of oblong tubers and its disease and drought tolerance. **'Chieftan'** isn't far behind, producing round potatoes with bright red skins and white flesh. This selection has great resistance to scab and other diseases. **'Tolaas'** is a mid-season producer, bearing large, smooth, white-fleshed potatoes with translucent skin. This one was bred for its adaptability to heavy and dry soils, and it stores for long periods once

'Kennebec' (above)

harvested. **'Burbank Russet'** is a large, flat, white-fleshed variety with shallow eyes. This potato has a great shelf life and is best grown in light, sandy soil. **'Banana'** is a fingerling type with yellow skin and flesh. Its vigorous growth results in heavy yields. **'Austrian Crescent'** is another fingerling variety, with tan skin and yellow flesh. **'Purple Peruvian'** is also a fingerling, but it is purple inside and out. **'Caribe'** produces a purple skin with pure white flesh in mid-season.

Problems and Pests

Potatoes are susceptible to a variety of diseases, including scab. Avoid planting them in the same spot 2 years in a row. Potato beetle is the most troublesome insect pest.

Radishes

Raphanus

Radishes are grouped into two categories. Spring or salad radishes, which include the familiar round, red radishes and icicle radishes, are used in salads. Winter radishes, which include Oriental or daikon radishes and Spanish radishes, are eaten raw or cooked and can be pickled. The spicy pods of some Oriental radishes are also popular in salads. Radishes are a great spicy addition to a variety of recipes far beyond the standard salad, so expand your vegetable garden and culinary horizons and give them a try.

Starting

Direct sow seeds in spring, as soon as the soil warms up a bit and can be worked. Plants tolerate light frost. Successive, smaller plantings can be made every 2 weeks to ensure a steady supply of radishes. Daikon and other radishes that can be stored for winter can also be started in mid-summer to be harvested in fall.

Growing

Radishes grow well in **full sun** or **light shade**. The soil should be of **average fertility, loose, humus rich, moist** and **well drained**. Heavy or rocky soils cause the roots to be rough, woody and unpleasant tasting. Radishes sprout and mature quickly; some varieties are ready to harvest within a month.

Harvesting

Spring radishes should be picked and eaten as soon as the roots develop. The flavour and texture deteriorates quickly if they are left in the ground or stored for too long.

Winter radishes are usually started in summer to be ready for harvest in late fall. They can be stored like carrots, in moist sand in a cool, dry location. They can also be pickled.

Tips

Easy to grow and a great addition to salads, radishes are also great nurse plants. If planted with mature plants or those that are small-seeded or slow to germinate, such as parsnips and carrots, radishes will shade out weeds and reduce evaporation.

Radishes tend to bolt in hot weather, causing the roots to develop an unpleasantly hot flavour. Choose icicle types for your summer growing because they are more tolerant of hot weather than the round, red varieties.

Radishes are related to cabbage, broccoli and mustard.

Because of their leafy, low-growing habit, these plants make interesting edging plants for borders and are unique additions to container plantings. Use radishes for a quick-growing spring display that will be replaced by other plants once the weather warms up.

Recommended

R. sativus forms a low clump of leaves. The edible roots can be long and slender or short and round; the skin can be rosy red, purple, green, white or black. The following are some of the more standard selections. **'Cherry Belle'** is an extra-early variety with exceptionally short tops and bright red skin. **'China Rose'** and **'China White'** ('China Celestial') are from a series that dates back to the 1800s. Aside from the skin colour, this series produces 15–20 cm long roots, 5 cm in diameter, with smooth

skin and crisp white flesh. **'French Breakfast'** is a large, scarlet radish, oblong in shape with white tips. The flesh is crisp, juicy, mild and sweet. It is ready in 20 days. **'Mooli Neptune'** is ready in 28 days, producing pure white roots 25 cm long. **'Pink Slipper'** produces oval roots with deep pink skin and white flesh in 30 days. **'Sparkler'** is ready in 25 days, bearing white roots that change to pink closer to the leafy stems.

Novelty radishes, including the following, are becoming more popular. **'Black Spanish Round'** produces

Young daikon radishes (below)

round roots, 7–10 cm or larger, with crisp, white, spicy flesh and black skin. This hardy cultivar is an excellent keeper. It is ready for harvest in 53 days. **'Long Black Spanish'** is more rare than the rounded type but is highly sought after because of the great flavour this heirloom radish dishes out. It bears a 23 cm long root with blackish grey skin and pure white flesh that is pungent, spicy hot and crisp. **'Green Luobo'** is a green radish inside and out. It is an elongated type that is vigorous and quite large, with tender, moderately hot flesh. **'Mantanghong'** ('Beauty Heart') produces white-skinned, round radishes with bright purple flesh. The flesh is crisp, sweet and slightly nutty, and only slightly hot. **'Red Meat'** ('Watermelon') is another Chinese radish, with white and green skin and dark pinkish red

flesh. Only 5–10 cm around, this radish is sweet with a touch of heat.

R. sativus var. *longipinnatus* (daikon radish) varieties are as delicious and interesting as the more standard radish selections. They also tend to be more mild in flavour than black types, and larger in size than red and white types. **'New Crown'** is considered to be a deluxe variety of daikon. It grows 30–35 cm long and 5 cm wide, with snow white skin and pale green tops. **'White Icicle'** is an early daikon radish, ready in 20–30 days, bearing long, slender, white roots from tip to stem. **'Fire Candle'** is a crunchy and tasty radish, deep red in colour, resembling a carrot. **'Minowase Japanese'** ('Minowase Summer Cross') is ready in 50 days, producing white, tapered roots 40 cm long with a medium to hot flavour. **'Omny'** is ready in 60 days and grows 40 cm long. This selection is very slow to bolt and likes cool temperatures.

Problems and Pests

Flea beetles and cabbage maggots are common problems for radishes.

The greens, or tops, of most radish selections can be eaten just like beet tops or turnip tops. They're tasty fresh or steamed and are full of nutrients.

Rhubarb

Rheum

Like tomatoes, pumpkin and peppers, rhubarb
treads the fine line between fruit and
vegetable. We usually eat it in fruit dishes
and think of it more as a fruit, but
rhubarb is actually a vegetable.

Starting

Rhubarb can be started from seed sown directly in the garden (not recommended because of the time it takes for the plants to be usable), or crowns can be purchased in spring. If friends or neighbours have a rhubarb plant, ask them for a division from their plant.

Growing

Rhubarb grows best in **full sun**. The soil should be **fertile, humus rich, moist** and **well drained**, but this plant adapts to most conditions. Gently work some compost into the soil around the rhubarb each year, and add a layer of compost mulch. A fertile soil encourages more and bigger stems.

After 8–10 years in one location, you may find that the plant is too crowded to produce as freely as it

Only the stems of rhubarb are edible. The leaves contain oxalic acid in toxic quantities.

used to. To rejuvenate the plant, dig it up in early spring while it is still dormant. Don't worry about severing large

The leaves contain sodium oxalate, a chemical that safely destroys ozone-depleting CFCs, giving the deep green leaves a purpose beyond photosynthesis. An abundance of this plant could help to reduce our carbon footprint.

roots when removing the rootball from the ground. Using a knife or spade, divide the crown, or the top of the rootball, into several sections, such as into fourths or even smaller, making sure that each section contains at least one bud or "eye." Replant the sections into different locations. If you can't replant the sections immediately, store them in the refrigerator and rehydrate them by soaking them in a bucket of water for at least 6 hours before planting.

Harvesting

Begin picking rhubarb once the stalks are large enough to use and roughly the width of your finger. Harvest the stems by pulling them firmly and cleanly from the base of the plant. Cut the leaves from the stems with a sharp knife and compost or spread them around the base of the plant to conserve moisture, suppress weed growth and return nutrients to the soil. Rhubarb's flavour is better earlier in summer, and harvesting generally stops by late July or early August, when the stems start to become dry, pithy and bitter.

Do not harvest the stalks in the first year. Let the plant develop an established root system first. Harvest sparingly the second year—not more than half of the stalks. In the third and subsequent years, harvest freely.

Tips

Sadly, this stunning plant is often relegated to back corners and waste areas in the garden. With its dramatic leaves, bright red stems and intriguing flowers, rhubarb deserves a far more central location.

Recommended

R. rhabarbarum and **R. x hybridum** form large clumps of glossy, deeply veined, green, bronzy or reddish leaves. The edible stems can be green, red or a bit of both. Spikes of densely clustered, red, yellow or green flowers are produced in mid-summer. A few of the more popular varieties include **'Colossal,'** with huge leaves and stems, **'Crimson Cherry,'** producing bright red stalks, and **'Victoria,'** a popular forcing type that bears greenish leaf stalks that mature to a combination of red and green.

There is a wide variety of hybrids and cultivars to choose from, but here are a few that are known for unique characteristics. **'Canada Red'** is very popular throughout the country because of its ability to be great in all categories, including flavour, hardiness, colour and texture. It bears deep red stalks that are shorter and a little more slender than other seedling types, but very tender. **'Chipman'** ('Chipman's Canada Red') also produces delicious red stalks, slightly sweeter than other varieties. **'German Wine'** bears green petioles, similar to 'Victoria,' but 'German Wine' is more vigorous and intense in colour, usually resulting in green stalks with dark pink speckling. **'Mammoth Red'** ('The Giant,' 'Stott's Mammoth,' 'Mammoth') is a vigorous producer, resulting in plants 1.2–1.5 m deep, red stalks and large, green leaves. **'Sunrise'** is a pink

'Victoria'

variety with thick stalks, ideal for forcing. **'Valentine'** produces thick, dark burgundy stalks that retain their colour when cooked.

Problems and Pests

Rhubarb rarely suffers from any problems.

Although the flowers are quite interesting and attractive, you can remove them to prolong the stem harvest.

Rutabagas & Turnips

Brassica

How these root vegetables ended up with the likes of broccoli, Brussels sprouts and spinach as the most disliked veggies on any child's plate is difficult to figure out. I suspect that the methods of cooking are to blame, as they tended to be cooked until they were mush. Turnips and rutabagas have a sweet, buttery, nutty flavour for soups, stews or just on their own as a side dish to any meal.
Just be careful not to overcook them.

Starting

Young plants can be purchased at your local garden centre and planted after last frost, or you can sow seeds directly into the garden in spring. Plant turnips 15–20 cm apart, but give rutabagas up to 25 cm because they're in the garden longer and may need a little more space. Keep the seedbed moist until the plants germinate. Several small, successive turnip sowings will provide you with turnips for longer.

Growing

Rutabagas and turnips prefer to grow in **full sun**. The soil should be **fertile, moist** and **well drained**. The roots can develop discoloured centres in boron-deficient soil. Work agricultural boron into the soil if needed.

Harvesting

The leaves can be harvested a few at a time from each plant as needed and steamed or added to stir-fries but are best fresh when young and tender. They can be eaten when more mature as well but should be cooked. They're particularly good when cooked and served with mustard or Swiss chard leaves.

The roots can be used as soon as they are plump and round, but they can also be left in the ground so the first few fall frosts sweeten the roots. Dig them up, cut the greens off and let them dry just enough that the dirt can be brushed off, then store them in moist sand in a cold, frost-free

Turnips are strong and resilient plants; however, there is a line that should not be crossed. Don't let the plants dry out for long periods, as this will adversely affect the quality of not only the roots but the leaves as well.

location for winter. Turnips do not store as well or as long as rutabagas.

Tips

Both rutabagas and turnips produce large, bushy clumps of blue-green foliage and can be included in the middle of a border where, though they aren't particularly showy, they provide an attractive, contrasting background for other plants.

Recommended

B. napus (rutabaga, swede, winter turnip, yellow turnip) forms a large clump of smooth, waxy, blue-green leaves. The roots are most often white with purple tops, and most have yellow flesh, but white-fleshed varieties are available. Rutabagas are generally larger than turnips and take longer to mature. A few varieties are usually on the market.

'**Laurentian**' and its many variations are commonly available and
are popular because they store well.
Choose a variety that is clubroot
resistant if this disease is common
in your region. '**Laurentian Golden**'
has smooth skin and light yellow
flesh and is a good keeper. '**Lizzy**'
produces purple-topped, yellow-
fleshed roots with a sweet, nutty
flavour, and '**Marian**' is a vigorous
grower. '**Magres**' is known for its
delicious, rich flavour, and '**Virtue**'
has red skin and sweet, yellow flesh.
'**American Purple Top**' is a common
variety with sweet, fine-grained,
yellow flesh. The flesh turns bright
orange when cooked. '**Helenor**' is
a strong producer with golden flesh
and red-skinned shoulders. '**Wil-
helmsburger**' ('German Green Top')
is a vigorous, disease-resistant heirloom variety with golden flesh and

The rutabaga originated in Europe and has been in cultivation for over 4000 years.

green shoulders. **'York'** is good for storing and is clubroot resistant.

B. rapa (turnip, summer turnip) is a biennial, very close to rutabaga in appearance. It often produces a large, rounded root but is also available in smaller varieties. The root, or swelling, grows at the surface of the soil with the top third exposed above ground level. This top is often purple-skinned, while the bottom two-thirds is white. The

flesh is often white or yellowish white. The leaves are rougher and hairier than rutabaga leaves. **'Early Purple Top White Globe'** and **'White Lady'** are popular cultivars. **'Just Right'** is ready in 70 days, producing white roots, inside and out. The rounded roots are slightly smaller than most and mild in flavour. **'Bianca Colleto Viola,'** which translates to "white turnip with a red collar," is from Italy and has excellent flavour. It produces a large, slightly elongated root with red shoulders in mid-season. **'Gold Ball'** is very similar to a rutabaga, with its yellow flesh and smooth, yellow skin. **'Hinona Kabu'** is an unusual turnip, with elongated, 3–5 cm diameter, 35 cm long roots. This Japanese variety has purple shoulders, and the greens are as delicious as the root. **'Milan'** is a baby turnip with a buttery flavour, bright red shoulders and white bottoms. **'Milan White'** has a similar

flavour but more of a semi-flattened shape and is all white, inside and out. **'Royal Crown'** is an early turnip, bearing globular, smooth-skinned roots with purple shoulders and creamy white bottoms, and deep green leaves. **'Oasis'** can be picked at any size. It bears super-sweet roots in 50 days. They can be eaten raw, whole like an apple or grated for salads and snacks. The flavour has been compared to that of a melon.

Problems and Pests

Cabbage root maggots, cabbage worms, cabbage white butterfly larvae, aphids, flea beetles, rust, downy mildew, powdery mildew and clubroot are possible problems.

There are turnip varieties grown for nothing but their edible greens.

Soybeans

Glycine

These beans have been popular for years in Asian countries. One common preparation method involves simmering the beans in the pod in salted water. The seeds are then eaten out of the pods. We know them as edamame. The seeds are also excellent roasted.

Starting

Sow seeds directly into the garden after the last frost date has passed and the soil has warmed up. Seeds can be planted quite closely together when space is at a premium, but ideally, give them 30–45 cm.

Growing

Soybeans grow best in **full sun** but tolerate some light afternoon shade. The soil should be of **average fertility** and **well drained**.

Soybeans contain all nine essential amino acids, have no cholesterol and are low in saturated fats and sodium. They are an excellent source of dietary fibre and are high in iron, calcium, B vitamins, zinc, lecithin, phosphorus and magnesium.

Soybean yields are very heavy, and 50–60 plants would be enough to feed a family of four.

Harvesting

Harvest the beans when the pods are plump and full but the seeds are still tender and green. The pods can also be grown to maturity and the beans dried for use in soups and stews.

Tips

Soybeans are very ornamental, with attractive leaves and plentiful flowers. They can be used to make low, temporary hedges or planted in small groups in a border.

Recommended

G. *max* is a bushy annual that produces clusters of large-seeded pods. There are several available soybean cultivars. **'Beer Friend'** is used primarily for edamame. **'Black Jet'** matures in less than 100 days and is a favourite when seasoned with garlic, ginger, molasses and cumin as a snack. **'Butterbean'** is ready in 90 days bearing bushy plants 60 cm tall with delicious, green seeds. **'Karikachi No. 3'** is the ideal edamame soybean, ready in 90 days. **'Manitoba Brown'** is a dark brown soybean that is incredibly vigorous and delicious, akin to the beans used in baked beans. **'Maple Amber'** is a Canadian soybean that is ready in 110 days, growing 90 cm tall and producing yellow seeds. Many other varieties are available, so look around and experiment.

Problems and Pests

Leaf spot, bacterial blight, rust, bean beetles and aphids can cause problems.

Spinach

Spinacia

Nutritious and versatile, spinach is useful in a wide variety of dishes. And it's effortless to grow, so you might want to consider adding this popular, leafy plant to your garden, even if you don't grow any other vegetables. In fact, it grows with ease in containers, with or without orna- mentals, so give it a try. After all, if Popeye likes it, it can't be all bad.

Starting

Direct sow spinach in spring as soon as the soil can be worked. Space the seeds approximately 20–25 cm apart. Several successive sowings in spring and again in mid- to late summer will provide you with a steady supply of tender leaves.

A young spinach plant can tolerate a light frost, but if temperatures are expected to fall below -5° C, you should cover it.

Growing

Spinach grows well in **full sun** or **light shade** and prefers cool weather and a cool location. The soil should be **fertile, moist** and **well drained**. Add a layer of mulch to help keep the soil cool because this plant bolts in hot weather. Most Ontario gardeners won't have to worry about bolting because our cool summer

The unrelated New Zealand spinach (Tetragonia expansa) is an excellent and interesting alternative to regular spinach. The leaves can be used in the same way, but the plant is far more heat resistant, upright and branching in habit and can be planted in summer as regular spinach begins to fade. It will grow quickly in the heat of summer and be ready for a late summer and fall harvest.

Smooth-leaved spinach has thin, tender, sweet leaves, while savoy-leaved spinach has broader, thicker, crinkled leaves that hold up better to cooking.

nights are ideal for growing spinach, but bolt-resistant varieties are also available.

Harvesting

Pick leaves, as needed, a few at a time from each plant. The flavour tends to deteriorate as summer heats up and the plant matures and goes to flower.

Tips

Spinach's dark green foliage is attractive when mass planted and provides a good contrast for brightly coloured annual and perennial flowers. Try it in a mixed container that you keep close to an entryway to make harvesting more convenient.

Recommended

S. oleracea forms a dense, bushy clump of glossy, dark green, smooth

Spinach beginning to flower and bolt

or crinkled (savoyed) foliage. Plants are ready for harvest in about 45 days. **'Bloomsdale'** produces dark green, deeply savoyed foliage. Many strains of this cultivar are also available. **'Correnta'** is a smooth-leaved variety with tender, dark green leaves. **'Scarlet'** is a smooth-leaved variety with dark red veins. **'Tyee'** is a semi-savoy variety that is very bolt resistant. **'Fiorana'** is an early variety, ready for harvest in 25–40 days. This is a great hybrid for successive plantings throughout the growing season. **'Regal'** is well-suited to dense plantings and is ideal as baby spinach. **'Olympia'** is ready in 46 days, bearing vigorous, dark green leaves that are slow to bolt. **'Unipack 151'** is a slightly later variety, ready in 50 days. It is a semi-savoy spinach with dark green, tender but thick leaves. **'New Zealand'** is a late variety with semi-crinkled leaves, and it will not bolt.

Problems and Pests

Avoid powdery and downy mildew by keeping a bit of space between each plant to allow for good airflow.

If grown successively throughout the season, 60 plants should be enough for a family of four.

Squash

Cucurbita

Squash are generally grouped as summer and winter squash. The groupings reflect when we eat the squash more than any real difference in the plants themselves. The squash that keep the longest and have the best flesh taste and texture when mature are grouped as winter squash. They develop hardened rinds in fall. Summer squash are tender and tasty when they are immature but tend to become stringy and sometimes bitter when they mature, and they don't keep as well.

Starting

Start seeds in peat pots indoors 6–8 weeks before the last frost date. Keep them in as bright a location as possible to reduce stretching. Plant out or direct sow after the last frost date and once the soil has warmed up. Plant on mounds of soil to ensure there is good drainage away from the base of the plant.

Spacing for seeds or plants will depend on the particular squash you are growing; check the seed packet or plant tag for specifics. Generally, though, squash require a lot of space, roughly 60–90 cm. If space is at a premium, some selections can be grown vertically, provided they have adequate support.

Growing

Squash grow best in **full sun** but tolerate light shade from companion plants. The soil should be **fertile, humus rich, moist** and **well drained**. Mulch well to keep the soil moist. Put mulch or straw under developing fruit of pumpkins and other heavy winter squash to protect the skin while it is tender.

Squash generally need a long, warm summer to develop well. Gardeners in cooler areas will want to choose species and cultivars that mature in a shorter season.

Essential to growing squash successfully is fertilizing with compost tea or liquid fish fertilizer every 2–3 weeks.

Don't worry if some of your summer squash are too mature or your winter squash are not mature enough. Summer squash can be cured and will keep for a couple of months. They are still useful for muffins and loaves. Immature winter squash can be harvested and used right away; try them stuffed, baked or barbecued.

Harvesting

Summer squash are tastiest when picked and eaten young. The more you pick, the more the plants will produce. Cut the fruit cleanly from the plant, and avoid damaging the leaves and stems to prevent disease and insect problems.

Winter squash should be harvested carefully, to avoid damaging the skins, just before the first hard frost. Allow them to cure in a warm, dry place for a few weeks until the skins become thick and hard. They can then be stored in a cool, dry place, where they should keep all winter. Check them regularly to be sure they aren't spoiling.

Tips

Mound-forming squash, with their tropical-looking leaves, can be added to borders as feature plants. The heavy-fruited, trailing types will wind happily through a border

of taller plants or shrubs. Small-fruited, trailing selections can be grown up trellises. All squash can be grown in containers, but the mound-forming and shorter-trailing selections are usually most attractive; the long-trailing types end up as a stem that leads over the edge of the container.

Recommended

Squash plants are generally similar in appearance, with medium to large leaves held on long stems. Plants are trailing in habit, but some form very short vines, so they appear to be more mound forming. Bright yellow, trumpet-shaped, male and female flowers are borne separately but on the same plant. Female flowers can be distinguished by their short stem and by the juvenile fruit at the base of the flower. Male flowers have longer stems.

Summer squash are available in a variety of shapes and colours, including:

- scallop or patty pan, which are rounded, no bigger than the palm of your hand and have soft skins, often in pale colours, and white flesh

- constricted neck squash, which are thinner at the stem than the blossom end and usually have yellow skin and white flesh; also known as crookneck or straightneck squash, depending on whether the stem is straight or crooked

- cylindrical to club-shaped, which are usually varying shades of green but may be yellow- or white-skinned, with white flesh; also known as Italian marrow.

Winter squash are also available in a variety of types but are not really divided into groups. They do vary greatly in shape, size, texture and colour, but they all have hard or thick rinds and thick but tender flesh, often sweet and fibrous.

There are four species of squash commonly grown in gardens. They vary incredibly in appearance and can be smooth or warty, round, elongated or irregular. They can be dark green, tan, creamy white or bright orange, solid,

striped or spotted. The size ranges from tiny, round zucchini that would fit in the palm of a child's hand to immense pumpkins that could hold two or three children. Experiment with different types to find which ones grow best in your garden and which ones you like best.

C. argyrosperma (*C. mixta*) includes cushaw squash and is not very well known. These plants generally take 100 days or more to mature. Some are grown for their edible seeds,

'Butternut' (above)

while others are used in baking and are good for muffins, loaves and pies. There aren't a lot of varieties to choose from, but two are definitely worth mentioning. **'Winter Cushaw'** is a very large squash with a crooked neck, green skin with creamy white stripes and speckles, and a slightly sweet, yellow flesh. **'Green Striped'** is very disease resistant and can grow up to 5.5 kg.

C. maxima includes buttercup squash, hubbard and kabocha. These plants generally need 90– 110 days to mature. They keep very well, often longer than any other

squash, and have sweet, fine-textured flesh. The list of varieties is endless, but here are a few of the best or most interesting. **'Buttercup'** has a dark green rind with silvery grey lines, and dark yellow flesh that is sweet and nutty and similar to sweet potato in texture. **'Sweet Mama'** is also a buttercup squash, with striped green skin and sweet, yellow flesh. **'Ambercup'** is a kabocha variety with streaked orange skin and orange flesh, and **'Hakkori,'** also a kabocha, has deep green skin and orange, extremely sweet flesh.

C. moschata includes butternut squash and generally needs 95 or more days to mature. These squash keep well and are popular baked or for soups and stews. An endless array of varieties is readily available, including **'Butternut,'** which bears bottle-shaped, creamy brown fruits with orange-yellow flesh that is nutty in flavour. **'Butternut Supreme'** also

has a bulbous base with an elongated neck, tan skin and yellow flesh, but in a bigger size and higher yields. **'Waltham Butternut'** is a late variety with dark yellow flesh, tan skin and a blocky base.

C. pepo is the largest group of squash and includes summer squash, such as zucchini, and winter squash, such as pumpkins, acorn squash, spaghetti squash, dumpling squash and gourds. Summer squash are ready to harvest in 45–50 days, and the winter squash in this group take from 70–75 days for acorn and spaghetti squash to 95–120 days for some of the larger pumpkins. Being the largest and most diverse group, there are countless varieties to choose from.

Examples of summer squash include the following. **'Defender'** is an early, medium-sized zucchini variety that is highly disease resistant and mild in flavour. **'Black Forest'** is a climbing

squash, ideal for containers. It bears dark green, cylindrical, 15 cm fruits in great abundance. **'Midnight'** is a very compact, bushy squash, also perfect for containers. It produces spine-free stems and leaves for an easier harvest of the slightly speckled fruits. **'One Ball'** is an early variety, bearing round, yellow fruits with white flesh,

6–8 cm across. **'Eight Ball'** is similar but with green flesh. **'Early Prolific Straightneck'** is a vigorous squash, ready for harvest when the fruits are 10–30 cm long. The flesh is tender and delicious. **'Sunny Delight'** is an early variety of a scallop or mini squash, round, flat and small enough to hold in the palm of your hand. It has bright yellow, thin, edible skin and tender flesh. **'Vegetable Marrow White Bush'** is considered unusual because of its white skin. It resembles a zucchini in shape but is creamy yellow when mature.

The following are some of the most interesting and reliable winter pumpkin selections. **'Big Max'** is a huge, round, pinkish orange pumpkin, reaching diameters of 1.8 m and weights of 45 kg or more if left to mature in the right environment. **'Freaky Tom'** has a heavily warted, dark orange rind that is great for Halloween carving. **'Jack O'Lantern'** is another pumpkin ideal for carving because of its smooth, firm, bright orange rind. **'Small Sugar'** is a super-sweet baking squash in the pumpkin group, maturing to 15–20 cm across. **'Rouge Vif d'Etamps'** ('Cinderella') is an heirloom squash. It bears vivid, red-skinned, flattened, heavily ribbed fruits, up to 7 kg in size, with moist, orange flesh ideal for pies.

Acorn squash, from the winter grouping, include **'Batwing Acorn,'** ready in 75 days with a patchy dark orange and green, rounded and ribbed rind, and **'Honeybear,'** a variety with dark green skin and sweet flesh in a mini form, averaging 0.5 kg each.

Problems and Pests

Problems with mildew, cucumber beetles, stem borers, bacterial wilt and whiteflies can occur. Ants may snack on damaged plants and fruit, and mice will eat and burrow into squash for the seeds in fall.

Sunchokes
Jerusalem Artichokes

Helianthus

Sunchokes, of the sunflower family, are a native species that develop edible tubers, which taste like artichokes, radishes or waterchestnuts, depending on who is describing the flavour. Known as "sun roots" prior to European settlers' arrival, these tubers were a diet staple for First Nations, and later for Europeans as well. The other common name, Jerusalem artichoke, was thought to have derived from the idea that the sunchokes were food for the "new Jerusalem."

Starting

Sunchokes can be sown directly into the garden, 30–90 cm apart depending on how much space is available, in spring around the last frost date. Water well until the plants become established. Sunchokes are perennial and will grow back each year as long as you leave some of the tubers in place in fall.

Growing

Sunchokes grow best in **full sun**. The soil should be of **average fertility, humus rich, moist** and **well drained**, though plants adapt to a variety of conditions. They become quite drought tolerant as summer progresses.

Harvesting

Sunchoke tubers are usually ready to harvest around the time of the first frost in fall. They should be

stored in a cool, dry, well-ventilated area. They have only a small trace of starch but contain plenty of inulin, which turns into fructose when they're stored in a cold room, refrigerator or the ground. In fact, once the tubers are cooled in storage, they develop a much sweeter taste.

Tips

Sunchokes are crunchier and sweeter than potatoes, with a hint of artichoke. They can be boiled, baked, fried, steamed, stewed or eaten raw. They cook more quickly than potatoes do and become mushy if overcooked.

Recommended

H. tuberosus is a tall, bushy, tuberous perennial. It grows 1.8–3 m tall and spreads 60 cm–1.2 m. Bright yellow flowers are produced in late summer and fall. There are a great many sunchokes to choose from, but here are some of the ones that stand

out. **'Mulles Rose'** produces large, white tubers with rose-purple eyes. **'Stampede'** is an early yielding, large sunchoke, ready in 90 days with white flesh. **'Fuseau'** is a long, straight tuber, knob-free with white flesh. **'Sugarball'** originated in Hungary and is super sweet. **'Sakhalinski Rouge'** produces branching, smooth tubers flushed with violet and with fewer knobs. **'Boston Red'** has large, rosy red tubers with smooth outer skin. **'Dwarf Sunray'** bears tender, crisp tubers that do not require peeling. **'Golden Nugget'** has golden tubers that resemble carrots, tapered at the tips. **'Jack's Copperclad'** is an heirloom variety and is difficult to find, but well worth the search. It bears plump, knobby tubers with dark copper or rose-purple skin and sweet flesh.

Problems and Pests

Sunchokes are generally problem free.

Sunchokes store energy in the tubers as a carbohydrate called inulin, rather than as starch. They are filling, but the energy is not readily absorbed by the body and does not affect blood sugar levels, making these tubers useful for people with diabetes or who are trying to lose weight.

Sweet Potatoes

Ipomoea

There has always been a little confusion where the sweet potato is concerned. It is consistently confused with the yam, and the names are used interchangeably depending on where you are. So which is which, you ask? The sweet potato, *Ipomoea batatas*, often has moist, sweet, orange-red flesh, while the yam, *Dioscorea* species, often has dry, starchy, yellowish white, potato-like flesh. The sweet potato has a much wider appeal to gardeners and chefs alike because of its versatility and delicious flavour.

Starting

Sweet potatoes are grown from slips, or rooted cuttings, not seed. The slips can be purchased from a garden centre, local farm, mail-order company or online vegetable supplier. Once you've grown a crop of sweet potatoes, you can also overwinter the roots for the next year's crop. Don't bother with trying to grow slips from sweet potatoes bought at the grocery store because they are treated to prevent sprouting.

Lift the tubers from the soil once the vines begin to yellow or when they're still slightly immature. Use the tubers fresh from the garden or store them in a cool, dark location for up to a week, unless you're curing them for the long haul.

To produce the slips for the coming season, start approximately 3 months before the last frost date by placing a sweet potato in a glass that is half full of water. Only one-third of the tuber should be immersed in the water. Place the glass, or glasses, in a warm, sunny location to sprout. When the newly formed sprouts are at least 12–15 cm long, pull them off gently and set them into water or damp sand until they develop a root system of their own.

Once the slips are rooted, and hardened off, they can be planted out about 2 weeks after the last frost, once the soil has warmed. The night temperatures should be at least 15° C. Plant the slips to the first set of leaves, about 30–45 cm apart, in mounded hills in rows. The rows should be about 90 cm apart. Sweet potatoes can be grown closer

together; doing so will result in smaller but more tubers.

Growing

Sweet potatoes require **full sun** and at least 100 warm days and nights to produce adequate tubers. Even the lightest frost will kill the plants, so make sure not to plant the slips too early. The soil should be **moist** and **well drained**.

Hilling the soil helps to keep the tubers warm and improves drainage. Laying a dark plastic mulch over top of the mounds, with the vines poking through, will help colder region gardeners to raise the soil's temperature. Top growth may be slow to start, but once they get rooted in and the daytime temperatures heat up, their growth will become quite vigorous. Once the vines begin to develop, make sure to cultivate underneath, or lift them occasionally, to prevent the vines from rooting in, which will only create competition for the main set of roots. Otherwise, sweet potatoes are very self-reliant and require very little until harvest. Fertilize with compost tea, only if necessary, roughly 5–6 weeks after planting.

Harvesting

Sweet potatoes can be harvested as soon as they are large enough to use. For the best flavour, wait until the

foliage, or top portion of the plants, is killed off by a light or moderate frost. Once this has taken place, harvest the roots immediately. Remove the tubers carefully with a garden fork so you don't bruise them. Bruised tubers should be used first, while the rest can be stored for long periods.

If you're going to store them, they should be cured first. Let them sit in the sun for a day, separated and dry, then place them in a humid location out of direct sunlight for roughly 2 weeks. Once the curing stage is complete, store the tubers in a dry, cool location for up to 5 months.

Tips

Sweet potatoes are really a vegetable garden kind of plant and should be planted in a hot and sunny location where they can grow on their own.

Recommended

I. batatas (sweet potato, yam) is a trailing perennial that produces deeply lobed, deep green leaves, funnel-shaped, violet flowers and tuberous roots with orange flesh and skin. There are a great many varieties to choose from, but the earlier selections are best for Ontario gardens. **'Select'** tolerates acidic soils and drought, stores well

and is super productive. **'Superior'** is very similar but with darker orange flesh. **'Beauregard'** is ready for harvest in 90 days, has large, tuberous roots, is quick to mature and is adapted to difficult locations. **'Beauregard Improved'** is a virus-free clone of the original with orange flesh and a more pronounced flavour. **'Centennial'** is ready as a baby baking sweet potato in 90 days, produces heavy yields and stores well. **'Georgia Jet'** is known for its enormous harvests and quality tubers. This selection is superb for baking because of its meaty, reddish orange flesh and sugary flavour, and it is ready in 100 days.

Problems and Pests

Sweet potatoes are rarely bothered by pests or diseases, but might experience leaf spot, sooty mould, black rot on the base of the stem or brown rot on the tuber itself. Rotate crops every 4 years to ensure the consistency of pH in the soil, thus discouraging fungal and bacterial problems. If flea beetles are a problem in your area, cover the tops of the plants with a floating row cover.

In good conditions, sweet potato tubers will ripen in 4–5 months.

Tomatoes

Lycopersicon

Tomatoes are likely the one plant that everyone tries to grow first when embarking on the experience of growing edible crops. They are quite possibly the easiest edible to grow. I was recently gardening with my dad when his neighbour came by to comment on our garden. She said she was just learning how to grow vegetables, and her first was a tomato plant. My dad commented on how easy it was, and to make sure she had some kind of support, like a tomato cage, then advised her to sit back and watch them grow, because that's all it really takes—that and a love of a delicious, nutrient-filled, sweet treat!

'Roma' (above)

Starting

Tomatoes can be started indoors 6–8 weeks before the last frost date or can be purchased in spring from nurseries and garden centres. Don't be afraid to plant seedlings and transplants very deeply. Roots will form along the buried stem, which allows for extra growing power and support. Bury the stem to the lowest set of leaves, or as close to the first set as possible. Spacing varies for the different selections, so check the seed packet or plant tag for specifics.

Growing

Tomatoes grow best in **full sun**. The soil should be **average to fertile, humus rich, moist** and **well drained**. Keep tomatoes evenly

When tomato plants were first introduced to Europe, they were grown as ornamentals, not for their edible fruit.

moist to encourage good fruit production. Except for the very small bush selections, tomatoes tend to be quite tall and are prone to flopping over unless stakes, wire hoops, tomato cages or other supports are used.

Harvesting

Pick the fruit as soon as it is ripe. Tomatoes pull easily from the vine with a gentle twist when they are ready for picking. Tomatoes can also be picked when green and ripened indoors, either left out in the open or placed in brown paper bags to speed up the process. This is often the case at the end of the season in locations with early fall frosts. It's important to harvest the fruits before a hard frost to prevent them from being damaged, hence the having to pick prior to ripening. Once picked, under-ripe tomatoes will keep indoors for weeks, if not months.

Tips

Tomatoes are bushy and have both attractive little flower clusters and vibrantly coloured fruit. Many of the selections grow well in containers and can be included in patio gardens and hanging baskets, particularly those varieties that produce cherry or grape tomatoes.

Bush is used interchangeably with determinate to describe plants with fruit that is set roughly all at once on short plants, whereas vine means indeterminate, or when fruit sets over a longer time on tall-growing plants.

Recommended

L. lycopersicum are bushy or vine-forming annuals with pungent, bristly leaves and stems. Determinate plants grow a specific height and are generally short enough to not need staking. Indeterminate plants continue to grow all summer and usually need staking. Clusters of yellow flowers are followed by fruit from mid-summer through to the first frost. Fruits ripen to red, orange, pink or yellow and come in many shapes and sizes. Beefsteak tomatoes

produce the largest fruit, and cherry tomatoes produce the smallest fruit. There is an endless array of tomato varieties to choose from, so experiment with a few each year.

Some of the best and unusual cherry tomato varieties include the following. **'Sugary'** is an All America Selections winner that produces cherry tomatoes reminiscent of the Roma type, with orange-red skin. **'Black Cherry'** is an indeterminate tomato with blackish purple skin and sweet, dark red flesh. **'Maskotka'** is a bush or basket form tomato, meaning that the growth is dense, compact and ideal for containers. The fruits are produced on thick stems that tumble over the edge for a heavy crop of tiny, sweet fruits with a great resistance to cracking on ripening. **'Sungold'** is

ready in 95 days, bearing the sweetest tomatoes from seed on the market. They are thin-skinned, rich orange and bite-sized, in a cascading form. **'Venus'** is a compact variety in a bushy form, producing orange-skinned fruits. **'Vilma'** was bred for containers, producing 60 cm tall plants with loads of sweet, juicy tomatoes. **'Tumbler'** is an early variety, ready in 50 days, bearing 2.5 cm fruits that tumble over the sides of containers on long stems. **'Honeybee'** is a bright yellow cherry tomato that is exceptionally sweet, borne in clusters and ready in 60 days. **'Moncherry'** is a vigorous, mini cherry tomato producing heaps of little red fruits.

Roma and more standard varieties of tomato heavyweights include the following. **'Shady Lady'** is ready for

Tomatoes growing within the confines of a tomato cage for support

Tomatillos (Physalis ixocarpa) *are related to tomatoes, and the plants have similar cultural requirements. The fruit is encased in a delicate papery husk. They are ready to pick when the husk is loose and the fruit has turned from green to gold or light brown.*

harvest in 95 days. It is compact, producing medium-sized, sweet fruit. **'Mortgage Lifter'** is an indeterminate heirloom variety that produces large, well-shaped fruits with dark pink skin surrounding meaty flesh with few seeds. **'Principe Borghese'** is ready in 75 days, bearing determinate, meaty tomatoes that do not require staking. **'Stupice'** is another heirloom that can be harvested in 52–85 days, depending on how big you prefer the tomatoes to be. This variety is ideal for Ontario gardens, has high yields, is great in cooler weather and produces

indeterminate vines that can stretch up to 1 m, bearing small to medium fruits. **'Black Krim'** is a Russian tomato that bears slightly flattened, 10–12 cm fruits with dark greenish black shoulders and an excellent flavour. **'Roma'** is a classic tomato, used for sauces but also superb when eaten fresh. The 85 g fruits are pear to oval shaped with very few seeds. **'Lemon Boy'** produces 170–200 g fruits with yellow skin and flesh on an indeterminate plant. **'Fleurette'** has the looks of an heirloom but the qualities of a hybrid. It produces elongated, banana pepper–shaped, super-sweet fruits with green at the shoulder that disappears as they ripen. This pure oxheart tomato is the purest of European tradition.

'Green Sausage' is another elongated variety, sausage-like in shape and green with yellow-striped skin and green flesh.

Problems and Pests

Problems with tobacco mosaic virus, aphids, fungal wilt, blossom end rot and nematodes can occur.

Amaranth

Amaranthus

Amaranth is most commonly known to gardeners as an ornamental, but this drought-resistant plant provides one of the most complete sources of protein available in a seed. It is prolific, producing up to 10,000 seeds in a single flowerhead. Some varieties can produce up to half a million seeds per plant. Not only are the seeds nutritious and delicious, but so are the leaves, stems and young shoots.

Starting

Amaranth sprouts quickly when sown directly in the garden. Scatter seeds or plant in rows once all danger of frost has passed and the soil has warmed—mid-May to early June for most gardens.

Growing

Amaranth grows best in **full sun**. It adapts to most soil conditions, but it prefers a **fertile** soil. Spread a layer of compost on the soil before you plant to keep weeds down and to improve the soil. Although it tolerates drought, this plant grows best if the soil is kept fairly moist while it germinates.

Harvesting

The seeds usually ripen and fall about the time of the first fall frost. Several harvesting methods can be used. Over a drop cloth, large bowl or bucket, shake or rub the seedheads between your hands—wear gloves because the seedheads can be quite coarse. The seeds and plant bits are easy to separate because the plant bits are lighter and rise to the surface if you run your hands through the collected seeds and carefully blow a fan over them. The seeds are quite light, too, so make sure the breeze is not too strong. Leave the seeds to dry in a warm place before storing them in an airtight container. The seeds can be added to soups and stews, cooked as a hot cereal or side dish, or ground into flour and used in pancakes, muffins and breads. They can even be popped, like corn, for snacking.

The leaves can be harvested at any point throughout the season. The young shoots, stems and leaves can be steamed or lightly cooked for soups and stir-fries or used fresh in salads. Use them as you would spinach.

Tips

This plant is very tall and makes a good screen plant. It resembles giant celosia when in bloom and is indeed related to that popular annual. The flowers can be used in fresh or dried arrangements, but cutting the flowers will reduce your seed yield.

Recommended

Three species of amaranth are grown for their seed: *A. caudatus, A. cruentus* and *A. hypochondriacus*. These species are often tall, annual plants that produce large, plume-like clusters of red, purple, gold or green flowers. Several cultivars are available, including '**Burgundy**,' with purple-red leaves and large burgundy plumes; '**Golden Giant**,' with bright yellow stems and flowers that mature to deep gold; and '**Mercado**,' with dense, less plume-like, bright green flowerheads. '**Popping**' produces seeds suitable for popping, similar to popcorn, and '**Plainsman**' is a compact selection bearing burgundy seedheads followed by heaps of purple seeds.

Four species of amaranth are grown for their edible leaves: *A. blitum,*

A. cruentus, A. dubius and *A. tricolor.* The edible leaf species are very similar in appearance and form overall. Many selections are available for consumption. Keep in mind that most amaranth varieties have edible leaves and seeds, including most that are grown or sold as ornamentals. If you're unsure, don't go with a selection that you have no reliable information on, and go with your gut until you do.

Problems and Pests

Young plants look very similar to red-rooted pigweed, making weeding challenging. If red-rooted pigweed is common in your garden, start your amaranth plants in peat pots, then transplant them directly into the garden to make weed identification easier.

Amaranthus *species are reported to have a 30% higher protein value than other grains, including rice, wheat, oats and rye.*

Asparagus Peas

Tetragonolobus

Asparagus pea is likely unknown to most Canadian gardeners, regardless of where you are in the country, including Ontario. It is one of the lost edible garden plants from long ago. It's not an asparagus and it's not a pea. Records show that this plant was cultivated before 1569 for its dark red flowers that resemble those from a pea plant. It has become widely naturalized throughout parts of the world where it was once cultivated for food, and it is still grown for ornamental purposes. If you're interested in trying something new and different, give this lovely plant a try.

The pods are good steamed or stir-fried, alone or with other vegetables, or as a substitute for green beans.

Asparagus peas are best when steamed for 3–5 minutes. Drizzle with butter or an oil substitute, mash and serve on toast for a quick, nutritious snack.

Starting

Asparagus peas should be sown outdoors once the soil has warmed and the threat of frost has passed. The seeds should be planted 2.5 cm deep and 30–40 cm apart. Once they've germinated, thin the rows to 20–30 cm apart, allowing for adequate space for each plant to mature. Plants can be started indoors as well, approximately 4–6 weeks before the last frost to get an early start, or sown under cloches or in the greenhouse.

Growing

Asparagus peas prefer open locations with **full sun** and **well-drained** soil. If started indoors, transplant the hardened off seedlings to the soil when they're approximately 5 cm tall, spacing them 20–30 cm apart. Once the seedlings begin to grow, they may need low supports to keep the plants off of the ground.

Harvesting

The pods can be picked when they reach roughly 2.5 cm in length. Pick regularly throughout the production stage to promote additional growth and prolong the harvest. Picking the pods any later, or larger than 2.5 cm, results in stringy, inedible pods. If they do not bend with ease, they are no longer edible. Harvest in the evening after the leaves have closed so the pods are easier to see.

Tips

This sprawling annual has superb ornamental qualities. It can be easily integrated into a mixed bed in clusters, or grown in containers for something a little different.

Recommended

T. purpureus (*Lotus tetragonolobus, Psophocarpus tetragonolobus*; asparagus pea, winged bean, square podded pea, winged pea) is a sprawling annual that bears bright green, pea-like leaves and deep scarlet flowers, also similar to sweet peas or flowers from a pea plant. The winged pods are bright green, slim and short. They are as sweet as a garden pea, with a hint of asparagus, when picked young. This species grows quite low to the ground in a compact form.

Problems and Pests

Nothing really bothers this plant; it is considered to be pest free. There have been rare cases, however, of mildew. Birds may find this plant tasty, so caging or a floating row cover might be helpful.

Asparagus peas contain small amounts of protein, carbohydrates, iron and fibre.

Ceylon Spinach

Basella

This vine is known by many names around the world. It often has the word spinach attached, and for good reason. The young leaves and tips taste just like spinach, even though the two plants are very different and not related in any way. Ceylon spinach can be steamed, eaten fresh, added to soups and stews or just left to grow as an ornamental vine simply because of its aesthetic appeal.

Ceylon spinach is high in vitamins A and C, iron and calcium. It is also a rich source of soluble fibre.

Ceylon spinach can be used in soups or stews for flavour and as a thickener. It's also great in stir-fries.

Starting

The best way to grow this plant is from stem cuttings. You may not have access to cuttings, but if you do, use stems about 20 cm long. Trim away the larger leaves, insert the cuttings into small pots containing moist soil, and place them in a shaded location. Plant out rooted cuttings 2 weeks after the last frost, into the ground or into containers.

The seeded fruits fall from the plant and may self-seed readily. If seeds are available, soak them overnight before sowing them either directly into the ground after the last frost, or into containers.

Growing

Ceylon spinach grows best in **full sun** or **partial shade**. It thrives in high humidity and regions with hot summers. It prefers soils that are **fertile, moist** and **well drained**.

Harvesting

Harvest by cutting the young leaves and tips throughout the growing season for immediate use. Leave the older leaves and stems intact to promote further growth.

Tips

This vine can be grown along a support or fence in the vegetable garden, or it can be grown elsewhere in the garden where support is available. 'Rubra' is especially striking when grown as a vine on a trellis, arbour or pergola.

Recommended

B. alba (Ceylon spinach, Malabar spinach, red vine spinach, creeping spinach) is a perennial vine that produces bright green, heart-shaped leaves roughly the size of a quarter, in a vigorous manner. A single plant can reach up to 3.6 m tall. This soft-stemmed vine has a mild spinach flavour. It bears tiny, white clusters of flowers followed by purplish black, one-seeded berries. **'Rubra'** has reddish purple stems, green leaves and pink flowers. The red colour is lost when cooked.

Problems and Pests

This plant is prone to fungal diseases, particularly those that affect the foliage. Good air circulation can remedy this threat.

Ceylon spinach has a bit of a slippery texture and may take some getting used to. It can be eaten raw in salads or steamed as a vegetable.

Cress

Lepidium

Cress is a group of botanically unrelated plants grown for their sharp, peppery or mustard-like flavour. Broadleaf or curly cress (*Lepidium sativum*) and upland cress (*Barbarea verna*) are easier to grow than watercress (*Nasturtium officinale*), which requires very moist soil at all times. Most people know cress for its use in dainty little finger sandwiches with the crusts cut off, but as yummy as finger sandwiches are, there are lots more opportunities to use cress in your culinary repertoire. For our purposes, I'm focusing on one of the selections, *L. sativum*, because of its strong peppery flavour and ease of growth.

Starting

Broadcast cress seed over the surface of the soil and cover lightly with soil or compost. Seed can be sown in early spring as soon as you can work the soil or in late summer through fall. Continuous crops will provide you with fresh cress all season long, but starting a crop in the middle of summer may cause the plants to produce flowers too quickly without making enough growth to harvest.

Growing

Cress thrives in **full sun** to **light shade** in soil that is very **moist, well drained** and of **average fertility**. Sow in all but the hottest months to prevent the plants from bolting or going to seed.

Harvesting

To harvest, cut back plants halfway and they will resprout before flowering. When grown indoors purely for use as sprouts (immature plants), use sprouting trays just as you would for other vegetables and herbs. The sprouting trays don't require any soil and allow you to harvest the sprouts right at your fingertips all year long.

Cress should always be used fresh. If you can only grow it outdoors but would like to use it year-round, mince it and combine with water in ice-cube trays, and freeze for later use.

Tips

Cress is suitable for a spot in your herb garden, but ensure that enough space is left for a succession of crops throughout the growing season. Cress can also be grown in containers, which are ideal for growing cress indoors year-round. When grown for sprouts, cress can be grown or sprouted on wet paper towels between two layers of plastic or in a plastic container.

Cress is invaluable in salads, sandwiches and garnishes for its spicy flavour and finely curled, nutritious leaves. Cress is the perfect complement to egg dishes, including omelettes and quiche. Cress soup has an unusual and unique flavour. Cress can also be used as a substitute for spinach in dishes where a stronger flavour is required. Most meat dishes will benefit from adding a little cress at the end of cooking.

Recommended

L. sativum (broadleaf cress, curly cress) is a reseeding annual that produces deeply cut, lacy leaves on single, erect stems. Small, almost spherical flowers are produced only 3–4 weeks after sowing. It grows 15 cm tall and wide. Grow it on

a windowsill and harvest as sprouts, or broadcast it in the garden for a fast harvest (15 days). **'Bubbles'** produces leaves with ruffled edges and blistered surfaces that are quite hot to taste. This cultivar is also slower to bolt than others. **'Greek'** produces flat, dissected leaves that are spicy, sweet and nutty in flavour.

Problems and Pests

Cress selections rarely suffer from any pests, but mildew can be a problem during excessively hot days if your plant dries out completely, or during consistently wet weather.

All cresses are abundant in vitamins and minerals, containing iron, iodine, phosphorus and sulphur, all of which the body needs. The end result is not only medicinal but also cosmetic, as the nutrients act as a natural blood purifier, clearing the complexion and bringing a clarity and sparkle to the eyes.

Dandelions

Taraxacum

Ok, ok, I know what you're thinking. Dandelion? How could I possibly use a weed that's taking over my front yard? Well, the time has come to embrace the dandelion. Believe me, it's much easier than continuously fighting it, and eventually you'll find yourself touting the benefits of dandelions to all of your friends. Dandelions have been used medicinally for thousands of years, and they've been a staple in certain cuisines for almost as long. Every part of the plant can be used, clearly they're easy to grow, and they're even attractive. All you have to do is get past your negative associations with them. If you're willing to try one new thing this year, make it dandelions.

Do not eat dandelions that have been in contact with lawn fertilizers, herbicides or any other chemical contaminants.

Dandelion leaves are high in vitamins A and C and contain high levels of potassium, phosphorus, calcium, iron, copper and magnesium.

Starting

Dandelions can be sown outdoors 4–6 weeks before the last frost. Sow seed directly, and once they've sprouted above the soil, thin so they are 15–20 cm apart. Dandelions readily reseed themselves, but often in places where you'd rather they didn't grow.

Growing

Dandelions prefer **full sun** but will clearly grow in just about any light. As we all know, it doesn't really matter what type of soil they have, whether the drainage is adequate, or anything else for that matter, because these plants are incredibly resilient and tolerant of poor conditions. Add liberal amounts of compost to areas you're sowing if you plan on harvesting the roots.

Harvesting

A few weeks before harvesting the leaves, cover the plants with a dark, opaque fabric to block out most of the light, which will blanch the leaves, reducing the bitterness. The youngest leaves are the least bitter and most flavourful. Tender leaves can be picked throughout the growing season.

Pick the flowers when they are bright yellow and young. Use them fresh, making sure to remove all of the stem. To prevent the flowers from closing after cutting, place them in a bowl of cold water, taking them out just before eating or serving them.

The roots can be harvested at any time. Chop the dried roots into pieces 5 cm long and roast at 150° C (300° F) for about 10 minutes. Grind the roasted pieces, adding a quarter teaspoon to your coffee or hot chocolate for a new flavour.

Tips

Dandelions can be added to your herb garden, or they can be grown in a block or row in your vegetable garden. Dandelions can also be directly sown into containers for harvest closer to the kitchen.

Recommended

T. officinale is a hardy perennial that grows up to 30 cm tall. It produces long, deeply toothed leaves and deep yellow flowers on tall, hollow stems. The brightly coloured flowers quickly change to fluffy, airy seedheads that are easily taken by the first summer breeze. Over time, dandelions develop a deep and somewhat extensive root system. '**Thick-leaved Improved**' produces a tender, thicker leaf with less bitterness. '**Verte de Montgomery**' is very similar. Also consider using the wild varieties in your yard, which are probably just as tasty.

Problems and Pests

Dandelions are generally problem free.

The crowns are a delicacy when deep fried, and the roots can be used as a coffee substitute after being roasted and ground.

Fiddlehead Ferns

Matteuccia

These popular, classic ferns are revered for their delicious, emerging spring fronds and their stately, vase-shaped habit. The fiddleheads—the tightly coiled, new spring fronds—are only available for a few weeks in an entire year. They taste wonderful lightly steamed and served with butter. Remove the bitter, reddish brown, papery coating before steaming.

Fiddleheads should not be eaten fresh. They must be cooked first to remove the shikimic acid.

Starting

Crowns can be purchased and planted out in spring once the threat of frost has passed but are often available throughout the growing season, either as bareroot or potted stock. They are often sold as ornamental plants in the perennial department of your local garden centre or nursery.

This particular species of fern spreads by underground runners. Space the plants approximately 60–90 cm apart. New plants will develop from the main root and can be divided and moved or left in place.

Growing

Fiddlehead ferns prefer **light shade** or **partial shade** but tolerate full shade, or full sun if the soil stays moist. The soil should be **average to fertile, humus rich, neutral to acidic** and **moist**. Add compost to the planting hole to achieve a slightly acidic soil.

Moisture for ferns is rather critical. If the area is prone to drying out, consider using a thick mulch around the base of the plants, and possibly a soaker hose buried under the mulch, on a timer, to keep the roots and soil consistently moist. Leaves may scorch if the soil is not moist enough.

Harvesting

Let plants become established for a couple of years before you begin harvesting. Pick new fronds in spring just as they are beginning to uncurl, often in May, but varying depending on the length of your growing season, the last frost date and weather conditions. Mature ostrich ferns produce an average of 7 fronds. When picking fiddleheads, make sure to pick no more than 3 (no more than half) per plant to allow enough surface area for the plant to thrive throughout the growing season.

Tips

These ferns appreciate a moist woodland garden and are often found growing wild alongside woodland streams and creeks. Fiddlehead ferns are also useful in shaded borders and are quick to spread.

Recommended

M. struthiopteris (*M. pensylvanica*; ostrich fern) forms a circular cluster of slightly arching, feathery fronds. Stiff, brown, fertile fronds, covered in reproductive spores, stick up in the centre of the cluster in late summer and persist through winter. They are popular choices for dried arrangements.

Problems and Pests

These ferns rarely suffer from any problems.

Agriculture Canada determined that fiddleheads contain even more anti-oxidants than blueberries, are packed with omega-3 fatty acids and dietary fibre, are low in sodium and contain vitamins A and C, niacin, potassium, phosphorus, iron and magnesium.

Jicama

Pachyrrhizus

Pronounced HEE-ka-ma, this South American staple is not completely uncommon in a standard grocery store produce department, but it's the garden centre that is foreign to this tuberous root—at least in Canada. It may be because jicama requires roughly 9 months of hot weather for a good crop, but this requirement can be fudged somewhat by starting seeds or plants indoors long before they're ever to be planted out. A greenhouse doesn't hurt either. If you're feeling adventurous and are dying to try something new in the garden, jicama might just be the answer.

One of the most endearing traits of jicama is how it maintains its crunch even when cooked, similar to a water chestnut. The white flesh will not turn brown when exposed to the air, either.

This vegetable is delicious when eaten raw, sliced into salads and cold dishes. The flavour is mild and sweet with a crunchy texture.

Starting

Soak seeds in water overnight. After soaking, sow at least 2 seeds into each 10 cm pot filled with a potting mixture intended for seedlings. Place them under a grow light, on a warm windowsill or in a greenhouse, approximately 8–10 weeks before the last frost or earlier if your growing season is quite short. Thin the seedlings once germination is complete, leaving the strongest seedling in each pot to thrive. Up-pot regularly as plants outgrow their containers until it is safe to plant them outside. Support the plants if necessary.

Growing

Jicama prefers **full sun** and a fair amount of space. It can be planted out once hardened off and the threat of frost has long passed. If the soil is **rich with organic matter** and is **light** and **friable**, you may only need up to 4 months for smaller roots to mature, which are equally as tasty as the larger ones. Pinch out the growth tips if the plants are getting too big and to encourage bushy, dense growth. Do not let the plants go to seed; pinch out the flowers for added root production.

Jicama is a day-length sensitive plant, which means that the tubers are not produced until the days toward the end of the growing season are fewer than 9 hours long. These shorter days often coincide with the first frosts of fall, so you may need to provide protection to get tubers of a usable size. Greenhouses work; so do cloches and portable coldframes, which protect the foliage from the threat of frost while heating up the micro-environment around the plant itself, thus extending the season somewhat. Jicama can also be grown indoors under a light set-up. You will only be able to grow one or two plants, but it's definitely worth the effort. Cloches can also be used at the beginning of the season to hasten the process in the early stages and to acclimatize the young plants to the outdoors.

The plants will require support at some stage, if you want to keep them off of the ground. You can train jicama on a net, wire fence or bamboo tripod, but remember that if it is raised off of the ground, it might be impossible to protect it from frost.

Caution: similar to potatoes, any parts of jicama growing above soil level are toxic. Avoid eating any parts that were growing above soil level. If you see any parts of the tubers being exposed to the sun, hill with soil.

Harvesting

Dig the tubers once the foliage has died away, likely from frost in Ontario gardens, as late in the season as possible to allow time for the tubers to develop. Once harvested, store the roots in a cool, dark location to prevent them from getting woody and tough.

Tips

Jicama can be added to the vegetable garden or to large containers once it is large enough, but its ornamental value is limited.

Jicama can also be grown under polyethylene tunnel borders. These will heat up the environment surrounding the plants, while keeping pests at bay.

Recommended

P. erosus and *P. tuberosa* are the two species you will find in a seed catalogue, available for cultivation. They are also known as yam beans, or Mexican potatoes. These perennial vines are often grown as annuals. They bear heart-shaped leaves similar to bean plants, 3 to a cluster, and beautiful lavender, lupin-like flowers. The flowers are not borne until late in the season. The tuberous roots are rounded with a pointed tip. The white, firm, crispy flesh is covered by a rough, brown skin, almost like a hairy rutabaga. In Ontario gardens, expect the tubers to reach baseball size if started early indoors.

Problems and Pests

Weevils can pose a problem; otherwise, jicama is a pest-free plant.

In its native Central and South America, jicama is often served with a dusting of chili powder and lime juice.

Appendix: Companion Plants

The following plants, arranged in alphabetical order by common name, all provide certain benefits to other plants when growing in proximity to each other, and/or to the garden in general.

Alliums (*Allium* spp.): group includes onions, garlic, leeks, shallots, chives and others; repel and distract slugs, aphids, carrot flies and cabbage worms

Asters (*Aster* spp.): general insect repellents

Borage (*Borago officinalis*): deters tomato worms; companion to tomatoes, squash and strawberries, improving growth and flavour

Calendula (*Calendula officinalis*): repels and distracts nematodes, beet leaf hoppers and other pests

Caraway (*Carum carvi*): loosens soil where it grows; attracts parasitic wasps and parasitic bees

Carrot (*Daucus carota*): attracts assassin bugs, lacewings, parasitic wasps, yellow jackets and other predatory wasps

Chamomile (*Chamaemelum nobile*): encourages other plants such as herbs, including lavender and rosemary, to increase their essential oil content

Chrysanthemums (*Chrysanthemum* spp.): reduce the number of nematodes

Cilantro/Coriander (*Coriandrum sativum*): scent repels aphids, attracts tachinid flies

Dill (*Anethum graveolens*): attracts hoverflies, wasps, tomato horn

worms, honeybees, ichneumonid wasps, aphids, spider mites, squash bugs and cabbage looper

Fennel (*Foeniculum vulgare*): attracts ladybugs, syrphid flies and tachinid flies; repels and distracts aphids

Flax (*Linum usitatissimum*): deters potato bugs; companion to carrots and potatoes, improving growth and flavour

Geraniums (*Pelargonium* spp.): can be attractive to caterpillars, luring them away from adjacent plants

Horseradish (*Armoracia rusticana*): planted at corners of potato patch, will discourage potato bugs

Hyssop (*Hyssopus officinalis*): attracts honeybees and butterflies; repels and distracts cabbage moth larvae and cabbage butterflies

Larkspur (*Consolida ajacis*): protects vines against vine beetles

Lavenders (*Lavandula* spp.): general insect repellents; attract pollinating insects; provide protection against borers and mosquitoes

Lavender cotton (*Santolina chamaecyparissus*): general insect repellent

Lovage (*Levisticum officinale*): attracts ichneumonid wasps and ground beetles

Marigolds (*Tagetes* spp.): discourage beetles, nematodes and other pests

Mints (*Mentha* spp.): improve the flavour and growth of cabbage and tomatoes; deter white cabbage moths

Nasturtium (*Tropaeolum majus*): attracts predatory insects; repels and distracts cabbage loopers, squash bugs, white flies and cucumber beetles

Oregano (*Origanum vulgare*): repels and distracts aphids

Parsley (*Petroselinum crispum*): scent deters carrot flies

Peppers, hot (*Capsicum* spp.): produce a chemical that prevents root rot

Petunia (*Petunia* x *hybrida*): deters and distracts leafhoppers, Japanese beetles, aphids and asparagus beetles

Rue (*Ruta graveolens*): deters beetles in roses and raspberries; do not plant near cabbages, basil or sage

Sage (*Salvia officinalis*): deters cabbage moths and carrot flies

Tansy (*Tanacetum vulgare*): companion to roses and raspberries; deters flying insects, Japanese beetles, striped cucumber beetles, ants and squash bugs

Tomato (*Solanum lycopersicum*): when planted near asparagus, deters asparagus beetles

White alyssum (*Lobularia maritime*): reseeds frequently; helps to break up the soil, adding to organic content

Yarrow (*Achillea millefolium*): attracts predatory wasps, ladybugs, hoverflies and damselbugs

COMPANION PLANT RELATIONSHIPS		
Plant	Compatible Plants	Incompatible Plants
apricots	basil, tansy	
asparagus	basil, parsley, tomatoes	
beans	most herbs and vegetables	beets, cabbage, garlic, kohlrabi, onions
beets	broccoli, cabbage, chard, garlic, kohlrabi, onions	beans
broccoli	beans, beets, celery, chamomile, cucumbers, lettuce, mint, onions, oregano, potatoes, thyme, rosemary	
cabbage	Alliums, aromatic herbs, beets, celery, chamomile, chard, spinach, potatoes	beans, corn, dill, parsnips, strawberries, tomatoes
carrots	Alliums, bell peppers, grapes, lettuce, peas, sage, tomatoes	dill, parsnips
cauliflower	beans, celery	strawberries
celery	beans, broccoli, cabbage, cauliflower, leeks, nasturtiums, onions, spinach, tomatoes	parsnips

262 APPENDIX: COMPANION PLANTS

Plant	Compatible Plants	Incompatible Plants
chard, Swiss	beets, cabbage, lavender, onions	
corn	beans, cucumbers, melons, peas, potatoes, squash, tomatoes	cabbage
cucumbers	beans, broccoli, corn, lettuce, peas, sunflowers, radishes	aromatic herbs, potatoes
eggplant	beans, potatoes, spinach	
garlic	beets, lettuce, chamomile, parsnips, peaches, strawberries, tomatoes	beans, peas
grapes	basil, beans, carrots, geraniums, hyssop, peas	
kohlrabi	beets, onions	beans, tomatoes
leeks	carrots, celery, onions	
lettuce	broccoli, carrots, cucumbers, garlic, onions, radishes, strawberries	
melons	corn, radishes	
onions	beets, bell peppers, broccoli, cabbage, carrots, celery, chamomile, chard, kohlrabi, leeks, lettuce, tomatoes, strawberries	beans, peas
parsley	asparagus, tomatoes	
parsnips	beans, bell peppers, garlic, peas, potatoes, radishes	cabbage, carrots, celery
peaches	garlic, tansy	
peas	most herbs and vegetables	garlic, onions, potatoes
peppers, bell	carrots, onions, parsnips, tomatoes	
potatoes	beans, broccoli, cabbage, corn, eggplant, horseradish, marigolds, parsnips	cucumbers, peas, squash, sunflowers, tomatoes, turnips
radishes	cucumbers, lettuce, melons, nasturtiums, parsnips, peas	hyssop
spinach	cabbage, celery, eggplant, strawberries	
squash	corn, nasturtiums	potatoes
strawberries	beans, borage, garlic, lettuce, onions, spinach	cabbage, cauliflower
tomatoes	asparagus, carrots, celery, chives, corn, marigolds, nasturtiums, onions, parsley	cabbage, cucumbers, fennel, kohlrabi, potatoes
turnips	peas	potatoes

Glossary

Acid soil: soil with a pH lower than 7.0

Alkaline soil: soil with a pH higher than 7.0

Annual: a plant that germinates, flowers, sets seeds and dies in one growing season

Basal leaves: leaves that form from the crown, at the base of the plant

Blanching: to deprive a plant or part of a plant of light, resulting in a pale colour and usually a milder flavour

Bolting: when a plant produces flowers and seeds prematurely, usually rendering the plant inedible

Bract: a special, modified leaf at the base of a flower or inflorescence; bracts may be small or large, green or coloured

Cross-pollination: the pollination of one plant by a closely related one. Undesirable if the resulting seeds or fruit lack the expected qualities; beneficial if an improved variety results

Crown: the part of the plant at or just below soil level where the shoots join the roots

Cultivar: a cultivated plant variety with one or more distinct differences from the species, e.g., in flower colour or disease resistance

Damping off: fungal disease causing seedlings to rot at soil level

Deadhead: removing spent flowers to maintain a neat appearance and encourage a long blooming season

Diatomaceous earth: an abrasive dust made from the fossilized remains of diatoms, a species of algae; the scratches it makes on insect bodies causes internal fluids to leak out, and the insects die of dehydration

Direct sow: to sow seeds directly into the garden

Dormancy: a period of plant inactivity, usually during winter or unfavourable conditions

Double flower: a flower with an unusually large number of petals

Drought resistant: can withstand drought for a long time

Drought tolerant: can withstand drought conditions, but only for a limited time

Genus: a category of biological classification between the species and family levels; the first word in a scientific name indicates the genus

Half-hardy: a plant capable of surviving the climatic conditions of a given region if protected from heavy frost or cold

Harden off: to gradually acclimatize plants that have been growing in a protected environment to a harsher environment

Hardy: capable of surviving unfavourable conditions, such as cold weather or frost, without protection

Humus: decomposed or decomposing organic material in the soil

Hybrid: a plant resulting from natural or human-induced cross-breeding between varieties, species or genera

Inflorescence: an arrangement of flowers on a single stem

Invasive: able to spread aggressively and outcompete other plants

Loam: a loose soil composed of clay, sand and organic matter, often highly fertile

Microclimate: an area of beneficial or detrimental growing conditions within a larger area

Mulch: a material (e.g., shredded bark, pine cones, leaves, straw) used to surround a plant to protect it from weeds, cold or heat and to promote moisture retention

Neutral soil: soil with a pH of 7.0

Node: the area on a stem from which a leaf or new shoot grows

Perennial: a plant that takes three or more years to complete its life cycle

pH: a measure of acidity or alkalinity; soil pH influences availability of nutrients for plants

Plantlet: a young or small plant

Potager: an ornamental kitchen garden, often laid out symmetrically with raised beds or low hedge-edged beds

Rhizome: a root-like, food-storing stem that grows horizontally at or just below soil level, from which new shoots may emerge

Rosette: a low, flat cluster of leaves arranged like the petals of a rose

Runner: a modified stem that grows on the soil surface; roots and new shoots are produced at nodes along its length

Seedhead: dried, inedible fruit that contains seeds

Self-seeding: reproducing by means of seeds without human assistance, so that new plants continuously replace those that die

Single flower: a flower with a single ring of typically four or five petals

Spathe: a leaf-like bract that encloses a flower cluster or spike

Species: the fundamental unit of biological classification; the entity from which cultivars and varieties are derived

Standard: a tree or shrub pruned to form a rounded head of branches at the top of a clearly visible stem

Subspecies (subsp.): a naturally occurring, often regional, form of a species, isolated from other subspecies but still potentially interfertile with them

Taproot: a root system consisting of one long main root with smaller roots or root hairs branching from it

Tender: incapable of surviving the climatic conditions of a given region and requiring protection from frost or cold

Tuber: the thick section of a rhizome bearing nodes and buds

Understorey plant: a plant that prefers to grow beneath the canopies of trees in a woodland setting

Variegation: foliage that has more than one colour, often patched, striped or bearing leaf margins of a different colour

Variety (var.): a naturally occurring variant of a species

Index

Boldface type refers to primary vegetable accounts.

Acknowledgements

The author would like to thank her friends and family for their support and encouragement over the years. She would also like to acknowledge those who allowed us to photograph their gardens, and those who carefully grew some of the vegetables for this book, including Connie Jacobsen, Becky Wandio, the Master Gardeners and staff from Devonian Botanical Gardens, Riverbend Gardens and Peas On Earth, local market and community gardens and farmers markets in Edmonton, and Inspired Market Gardens. She would also like to thank Nanette Samol and Sandy Weatherall for working so hard to get the images throughout the season. Many more people contributed to the making of this book, and she is incredibly appreciative of all of their kindness and hard work. Thanks and happy gardening!

The publisher would like to thank Master Gardener Coordinator Justine Jenkins-Crumb at the Devonian Botanic Garden for her tremendous organization of the growing of many of the vegetables featured in this book both at the Garden and at the homes of many Master Gardener graduates and students, and Paul Swanson for his photographic contribution to this project.

About the Author

Laura Peters is a certified, seasoned Master Gardener, garden writer and photographer with over 30 gardening books to her credit. She has worked in almost every aspect of the horticultural industry in a career that has spanned more than 20 years. She passionately believes in organic gardening and food security, and she loves to share her knowledge with fellow gardeners and environmentalists alike. She lives in Edmonton with her two cats Blackie and Luna, and gardens both on her condominium balcony and in her parents' gardens just to mix it up with a variety of settings. Laura is inspired by nature and hopes that you will become inspired to grow more of your own food, regardless of space, financial, time and skill restraints, because anything is possible and the rewards are priceless.